HISTORICAL PERSPECTIVES
ON PUERTO RICAN SURVIVAL IN THE U.S.

To future generations
of Puerto Ricans in the United States

Mr. Mario Rivera is a co-founder of the Taller Puerto Rico
in Philadelphia, PA. He was one of the early artists and print-makers
of Philadelphia and was responsible for pioneering
many efforts in art and culture.

Historical Perspectives on Puerto Rican Survival in the U.S.

Clara E. Rodríguez
Virginia Sánchez Korrol
EDITORS

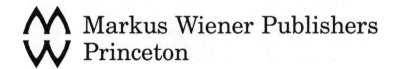 Markus Wiener Publishers
Princeton

For information write to: Markus Wiener Publishers
114 Jefferson Road, Princeton, NJ 08540

Library of Congress Cataloging-in-Publication Data

Historical perspectives on Puerto Rican survival in the United States/
    Clara E. Rodríguez and Virginia Sánchez Korrol, editors.
    Updated ed. of: The Puerto Rican Struggle, 1984.
    Includes bibliographical references
    ISBN 1-55876-117-9 hardcover
    ISBN 1-55876-118-7 paperback
    1. Puerto Ricans—United States.   2. United States—Ethnic
rela tions.   I. Rodríguez, Clara E., 1994-   .   II. Sánchez Korrol,
Virginia.   III. Puerto Rican struggle.
E184.P85H56   1996
305.868'7295073—dc20   96-17005
                                             CIP

Markus Wiener Publishers books are printed in the
United States of America on acid-free paper, and meet
the guidelines for permanence and durability
of the committee on production guidelines for book
longevity of the council on library resources.

Contents

Preface to 1996 Edition

The Story of the Struggles Book

Conception

This early collection originated in a 1975 dispute between Clara Rodríguez (CER) and the publisher and editor of a then widely-known journal. The journal prided itself on its coverage of relevant urban issues but had done little by way of covering Puerto Ricans. The dispute took place at a professional conference, while both CER and the editor, a casual acquaintance, waited to be seated with separate groups at a restaurant. CER commented on the journal's lack of coverage of Puerto Ricans, particularly *by* Puerto Ricans. The editor responded, in an irritated and antagonistic fashion, that he didn't print anything by Puerto Ricans because he couldn't find any Puerto Ricans who could write. CER answered, "I know a lot of Puerto Ricans who can write." After a provocative exchange, a proposal evolved: if CER could find a group of Puerto Ricans who could write, the editor would consider a special issue of the journal on Puerto Ricans.

The fact that such a "threat/offer" was made was truly astounding at the time. Few publishers, if any, sought to publish works by Latinos. That there might be "voices" from this community having something to say had not yet dawned on the overwhelming majority of publishers in the social sciences. This is not to say that nothing had been published on Puerto Ricans. Quite the contrary. There had been a near-avalanche of social science literature *on* Puerto Ricans by non-Puerto Ricans during this period (Rodríguez, 1995). But these included a smattering of works in English by Puerto Ricans. As Gordon Lewis (1963) early pointed out, Puerto Ricans held the dubious distinction of being one of the most researched and least understood peoples in the United States.

A number of factors contributed to (and continue to contribute towards) making Puerto Rico a favored research site. In addition to its warm, inviting, tropical climate there exists the reality of the political ease (and intellectual advantage) of researching a country that is part of the United States, yet culturally and linguistically different (Lewis, 1966). Thus, of 20 major social science studies on Puerto Ricans undertaken between 1938 and 1970, only one—that by Elena Padilla (1958)—was written by a Puerto Rican.[1] Although there were English-language works by Puerto Ricans on Puerto Ricans (e.g., Fernández Méndez, 1972; Seda Bonilla, 1973), they were few in number and, with scant exceptions, were not seriously considered by the intellectual community during this period.

Coinciding with the curious restaurant repartee between the editor and CER was a growing awareness among many of the scholars teaching Puerto Rican Studies of the need for better teaching materials for classroom use. Needed were English-language materials that addressed the perceived realities, needs, and past experiences of the students in the classroom. Unfortunately, too many of the resources that existed in English tended to ignore issues of Puerto Rican political sovereignty; obfuscated or viewed as benign the political relationship between Puerto Rico and the United States; focused exclusively on the island without allowing for comparative perspectives; misrepresented, underrepresented, or totally ignored indigenous histories and voices; utilized inappropriate contexts, categories, and concepts to examine Puerto Ricans; and lastly, generalized from extreme cases to the whole population. Although some studies were better than others, the works generally conveyed a strong sense of "otherness" in their depictions of Puerto Ricans (Rodríguez, 1995).

Other problems existed with much of the English-language literature on Puerto Ricans. A strong malthusian thrust, for example, viewed Puerto Rico's problems as the result of its overpopulation (Hernández, 1991c; History Task Force, 1979; and Hernández Cruz, 1988). At issue also was a preoccupation with race (Rodríguez, 1995) that often occurred within a more widely-applied deficit model. These studies tended to view Puerto Rico and Puerto Ricans as "a problem," or an expensive liability with few accomplishments or contributions. Also found in the literature was an implicit assumption that the history of the Puerto Rican community in the states was undistinguished and of fairly short duration. As part of this often unspoken deficit-assumption, there was a tendency to ignore issues and perspectives of concern to Puerto Ricans; and a disparagement of Puerto Rican language and culture.

Although a number of English-language works had begun to address many of the above issues (Figueroa, 1974; Maldonado Denis, 1972; Silén, 1971; and López, 1973), these works centered their analyses on Puerto Rico, particularly on the status question. Few critical works addressed Puerto Ricans in the United States during this period. The López & Petras (1974) anthology was one of the first to devote one third of the articles to "the Puerto Rican diaspora" in the states. Many, many dissertations had been written, but these were buried. What was evident to teachers and learners alike was that studies were needed that focused on issues that had been long ignored in the literature. Indeed, the practical reality for many faculty was that inordinate amounts of time and energy went towards translating, copying, searching for, and finally creating materials from various sources to use in, and customize to, a wide range of Puerto Rican Studies courses.

There were also people who could and wanted to write. Some represented emergent U.S.-raised, ghetto-grown, college-educated Puerto Ricans who challenged, or wanted to correct, the existing interpretations. They yearned to create materials that approximated the experience as they had lived it. Others had come from Puerto Rico and had further honed their perspectives in the states. They too wanted a voice. Others were non-Latinos, supportive of alternative views that were generally missing from the public discourse. All wanted to express their convictions, centering on issues that received little coverage at the time. Thus, the initial anthology was born out of need, threat, and an indignation over the lack of attention to the struggles and survival of Puerto Ricans in the United States. It was intended to contest the despair and deficit-driven models encountered in the conventional literature.

Birth

The subsequent story of the book's development paralleled in many ways the community's own struggles for survival. Originally, we proceeded with enthusiasm and determination. Almost all the articles we solicited were original *first* drafts by authors who had not published extensively. We had no funding, less time, and overwhelming competing responsibilities. However, as counterbalance, we held a strong conviction that the project was important and would fill a significant void in the field.

The Context Then.

The political-economic context within which this took place is also important to bear in mind. This collection first appeared in 1980, but it was begun in 1975. This was the year of the New York City fiscal crisis. Drastically slashed budgets eliminated the City University's traditional policy of free tuition and eroded the recently established open admissions policy. Both of these policies had enabled many Puerto Rican and other working class students to attend college. It was a time of ferment and change and many of our contributors (ourselves included) were living personally stressful lives within highly pressurized environments. Some were beset by administrative attempts to eliminate their programs, or their jobs and futures were in doubt.

Nonetheless, we pulled the articles together and sent them to the editor. To our dismay, he proceeded to pick and choose those he would publish, essentially invalidating our roles as editors of the collection. Obligated to present the perspectives of our colleagues and to maintain the strength of the collection in its entirety, we felt the publication of *all* of the articles was non-negotiable. Our enormous commitments of time and energy had been expended willingly with the understanding that these efforts would ultimately aid our community. It had been decided early on that all proceeds from the sale of the book would go towards the establishment of a student fund to assist further work in the field of Puerto Rican Studies. We decided to go elsewhere. Again with little expectation of interest, we wrote letters to publishers. Again, to our great surprise, one small publisher expressed interest and even extended a contract. A real book!

However, soon after we initiated this phase, our major, lead article was withdrawn because the collective to which the original contributor was responsible withdrew the article. This was a major blow because the lead article framed the ones that followed. We could not accept the publisher's contract. Despite our very real disappointment, we again sought alternatives. In 1980, the book was finally published by the Puerto Rican Research Consortium, a funded group that went out of existence shortly thereafter. Despite the book's popularity and success with students, it was at this point relegated to the nether world of similar works referred to by Stanford University's Curator of Chicano Studies as "phantom" works. These are (often historical) writings that are difficult to locate, and subsequently cease to exist.

Growth and Re-Birth

Our enduring commitment to present the voices of Puerto Ricans, and the demand of students, many of whom discovered their "history" for the first time in the Struggles anthology, continued and we signed on with another press dedicated to marketing books on Puerto Ricans. At first, this press made the volume available, but it too went out of existence and the book was again relegated to the world of the has-never-been.

It is because of this history of struggle and perseverance,

so like that found among many Puerto Ricans in diaspora communities, that we are pleased this book is being re-issued with appropriate updates. It is considered a classic in the field, one that has withstood the changes of style and retained its substance. It well represents the perspectives of this now-historic period. It continues to resonate with readers in part because it mirrors the experiences of other groups, both past and more recent immigrant groups; and in part because, when the authors wrote their essays, they spoke honestly about issues they cared about but others tended to ignore. As the introductions to the selections indicate, the anthology has also served as a spring from which other works have developed. The issues then addressed continue to be at the core of the discourse today, although there have been changes of venue, style, and address.

The "Great Divide"

The volume is also important because its history and contents represent an issue that is very much alive in today's world. This is the great divide that still exists between literature produced under the "ethnic studies" umbrella and that which is considered "mainstream," "academic" or non-ethnic—even though the central concerns of the works may be race and/or ethnicity. In the field of African-American studies, there has been greater cross-fertilization between these two camps. Note for example the works of Henry Louis Gates, Cornell West, bell hooks, and Toni Morrison, among others. However, in the area of Latino, Puerto Rican or Chicano Studies, this has been less the case. A Latino work that is termed "ethnic studies" is compartmentalized and it is believed to be implicitly less rigorous and less credible than a similar work that is *not* termed "ethnic studies"—and that may be done by someone who is not a member of, or has had very limited experience with, the group being studied.

To some extent, the "great divide" exists because ethnic studies scholars and writers are perceived to be activists or advocates. This may or may not be so, but it would certainly be in keeping with the tradition of many "others" who speak from the position of "other" because they are structurally and often culturally in the "other" position. To do otherwise would be too untrue to their reality. This tradition has been exemplified by numerous African American scholars, such as DuBois, and it is an important tradition that has been preserved in many Native American Indian writings as well (McLuhan, 1971c).

However, many more have not been recognized and others totally forgotten—perhaps because they were too much in the camp of activists or advocates. Not acknowledged, and thus not referenced; and so the trail to their work is a difficult one to find. Occasionally re-discovered by an enterprising graduate student, the presumption is often that there is something wrong with the scholar's work because why else is the scholar unknown. There is generally little to read that would disapprove this doubt. But for the watchful efforts of some modern-day scholars, who seek to retrieve this buried past, the work ceases to exist.

Jesse M. Vázquez (1992) articulates the issues surrounding the "great divide" well when he says:

> Many of these scholars that might have been considered "deconstructionists" or "post-modernists" in some circles; instead they were derogatively labeled "ghetto" scholars. Their work was sometimes de-valued, in large measure because their subject matter is de-valued. Others could and did study Puerto Rico and Puerto Ricans in great profusion during the 1940s, 1950s, and 1960s, but when Puerto Ricans started studying other Puerto Ricans it was seen as nothing more than the scholarly contemplation of one's own navel. If American scholars study American culture and society through American studies, this is considered serious scholarship. However, when a Puerto Rican researcher studies the Puerto Rican culture—any aspect of it—it was not seen as quite scholarly enough. (Vázquez 1992:1043).

Continuities

Despite the protestations of more traditional (and threatened) mainstream academics during this period, there has continued to be an energetic growth of interest in this new literature. This new edition of the book reflects the times from which it grew, and it also shows the developments since then.

The book was begun during the period of the late sixties and early seventies when many of the Puerto Rican Studies programs were in their formative stages. These programs rejected traditional approaches to learning about Puerto Ricans and defined new sources of learning that stemmed from within the Puerto Rican experience. Puerto Rican Studies discarded apologist and colonizing ideologies and designed new theoretical constructs within which fresh analyses about the Puerto Rican condition were generated. (Nieves, 1987)

Puerto Rican Studies was part of a new vision that reflected the changing times and place of Puerto Ricans and that early challenged the eurocentric perspectives on race and ethnicity—before multiculturalism became a byword. Puerto Rican Studies also argued for the application of knowledge to the resolution of community issues and struggles (Sánchez & Stevens-Arroyo, 1987). These were goals that were reflected in the collection then and these are the goals that many newer works articulate as explicit intentions.

What the Book Does:

Developed as a reader for Puerto Rican Studies courses, this early collection included articles that were vital to the Puerto Rican community at the time, but that were also generally ignored within more mainstream contexts. For example, articles on Puerto Rican women, the Young Lords, Latin music, the struggle for local political control, spiritualism, the struggles within the Catholic church, the Puerto Rican Day Parade, race within ethnicity, political activism, the economy, and a beginning critique of the conceptual models and methods used to "measure" the quality of life among Puerto Ricans made up this interdisciplinary volume. The attention to neglected issues was a first step in developing knowledge that would help in the resolution of community issues. The highly interdisciplinary nature of the articles, ranging from literary selections by non-academic writers to more traditional social science articles, would also come to typify other works subsequently done.

This reader also departed from traditional approaches in that it asserted that the experience of being Puerto Rican, if understood correctly, would enhance the work. Not that one had to be Puerto Rican to write accurately about the Puerto Rican community, or that being Puerto Rican was any guarantee of accuracy or insight; but that the experience of being Puerto Rican, if understood correctly, would enhance the work. Thus, it was no accident that many of those involved with this collection were second-generation Puerto Ricans or had experienced life in U.S. Puerto Rican communities.

Thus, the preface to the first edition stated that "the authors have been intimately involved in the issues they address and this sets their work apart from many traditional social scientists." The collection also endeavored to speak to "...the new reality of Puerto Ricans, their future, and a more accurate past than had been depicted in the traditional literature." (Rodríguez, Sánchez-Korrol, Alers, 1980:3) In so doing, this collection and others that followed attempted to put forth a more representative view by allowing those affected to speak for themselves from within their own framework of personal dignity.

The proceeds of this work will continue to be contributed to funds established at Brooklyn College, Fordham University, and the Rosa Estades award of the Puerto Rican Studies Association to aid in the further development of this field.

The Editors
New York City, 1996

Note

1. Although all of the 20 major works make mention of Puerto Rico
   in their discussion of Puerto Ricans, some focus specifically on
   Puerto Ricans in the U.S. These include, in order of publication,
   Lawrence Chenault (1938); C. Wright Mills, Clarence Senior, and
   Rose Goldsen (1950); Elena Padilla (1958); Oscar Handlin (1959);
   Dan Wakefield (1959); Clarence Senior (1961); Patricia Cayo
   Sexton (1965); Nathan Glazer and Daniel P. Moynihan (1970);
   Eva Sandis (1970); and Rev. Joseph Fitzpatrick, S.J. (1971). Both
   Handlin (1959) and Glazer & Moynihan (1970) focus on other
   groups as well as Puerto Ricans. Oscar Lewis's *La Vida* (1966)
   examines three families in Puerto Rico and two in New York and
   Christopher Rand (1958)'s work includes both Puerto Rico and
   Puerto Ricans in the U.S.
   Works that focus specifically on Puerto Rico but that are
   often cited in relationship to Puerto Ricans in the U.S. are:
   Vincenzo Petrullo (1947); David Landy (1959); Melvin Tumin and
   Arnold Feldman (1961); Gordon K. Lewis (1963); Julian Steward
   (1965); Anthony La Ruffa (1971); and Sidney W. Mintz (1972).
   Two points are evident from this listing of 18 books. With the
   exception of Padilla (1958) and the British Lewis (1963) all of the
   works were done by North American social scientists. (Padilla
   (1958) worked with a number of the other authors who had written on Puerto Ricans.) This listing and the bibliography make
   clear that many of these works were published by major presses
   and were conducted by persons who were either prominent at the
   time or were to become celebrated scholars.

Preface to First Edition

Readers seeking to educate themselves about Puerto Ricans have only a partial set of written materials from which to choose. What has been available up to now is limited in both English and Spanish. Specifically in need of expansion are materials in which Puerto Ricans born on the continent write about themselves or their compatriots on the island. The present collection begins to fill part of this void. It is historically significant because it constitutes the first published compendium of any appreciable scale containing social commentary and analysis by second-generation Puerto Ricans on their situation in the U.S. All the contributors to the volume are personally and/or professionally involved with the Puerto Rican communities in the U.S.

It is no accident that these first essays are devoted to the themes of struggle and survival, for these are our primary concerns. The focus of the collection is on the survival of Puerto Rican culture—our language, history, arts, preferences, practices, symbols, spirit and style—without which we would have no unifying identity as a people. This identity is under persistent attack by the forces of assimilation, not only in the U.S. but in Puerto Rico itself. The principal aim of the monograph is to highlight the process of assimilation and the means that Puerto Ricans have used in their struggle to survive as Puerto Ricans in the U.S. It also provides a forum for second-generation Puerto Rican perspectives that do not often find their way into print. We hope the volume will heighten the awareness of Puerto Ricans about their present condition and future prospects in the U.S.

Although the core of the collection falls generally within

the realm of the social sciences, a deliberate effort has been made to give voice to the concerns of the humanities. This means that some of the papers included are written from historical, philosophical or political perspectives. We consider the resulting variety to be a strength rather than a weakness because of the kind of audience we are interested in reaching. We expect that our readers will not be just Puerto Ricans, or students, or academics, or activists, or interested laymen, but all of these—and more. We thus anticipate that the variety of the collection will strengthen its appeal to a diverse audience. For this reason we also consider it important to cover some subjects at least briefly, with minimum documentation, rather than not at all. The papers vary greatly in their length, level of analysis, and use of statistics, notes and references.

The collection is published by the Puerto Rican Migration Research Consortium, Inc., a private, non-profit, tax-exempt organization with offices in Manhattan. Incorporated in 1977, the Consortium is the leading institution of its kind in the U.S. In keeping with its objectives, the Consortium encourages and facilitates research and publication by its members and other interested persons concerning Puerto Rican migration and its relationships to social institutions. It also serves as a center for research coordination and the dissemination of appropriate information to the Puerto Rican people, the public at large and policy-makers.

It is principally in the spirit. of these objectives that the Consortium has undertaken the publication of this collection, the first in a projected series of monographs. An additional reason for taking this action is that most of the papers themselves may be seen as written products of the Puerto Rican migration. What is said and how it is said constitutes relevant information about the state of the Puerto Rican community in the U.S.

Finally, we wish to acknowledge with gratitude the important contributions made by the authors and by a few other persons and organizations to the production of the volume. Publication was made possible by a grant to the Consortium from The Ford Foundation. Natasha Krinitzky, research assistant at the Consortium, performed many services useful in bringing the monograph to completion. Mario Rivera contributed the artistic work for the cover. A few of the papers in the collection have been published in earlier versions; permission to reprint parts of them is noted at appropriate points in the ensuing text.

The Editors
New York City

The Puerto Rican Struggle to Survive in the United States

by Clara Rodríguez, Virginia Sánchez Korrol
and José Oscar Alers

In the 19th century a migration began from the *campos* and *pueblos* of Puerto Rico to the northern metropolises of the United States. Puerto Ricans came as students and stowaways, as adventurers and revolutionaries, as field hands and factory workers. Forging niches in alien territories, they set about establishing communities and *colonias* which reflected those they had left behind. By 1910, Puerto Ricans in the U.S. numbered about 2,000; by 1930, conservative estimates placed their number at 45,000. By 1975, however, the Puerto Rican population in the U.S. had grown to 1.7 million (U.S. Commission on Civil Rights, 1976:19).

As early as 1925, Puerto Ricans in the New York *colonias* boasted a network of organizations and institutions designed to cope and facilitate interactions with the larger non-Latino society. The early steamship veterans laid the groundwork for what became after World War II an escalating and airborne migrant flow. This flow, from Puerto Rico to the U.S., peaked in 1952 when net migration surpassed 52,000 arriving in the U.S. Beginning with 1965, there was an increase in the number of Puerto Ricans returning to Puerto Rico. By 1969, the flow reversed — for the first time since the Great Depression more people went to Puerto Rico than came to the U.S. Current data show that the trend back to the island is continuing.

The migration flows between the U.S. and Puerto Rico have

Dr. Clara E. Rodríguez is Professor of Sociology, Fordham College at Lincoln Center, New York, N.Y. **Dr. Virginia Sánchez Korrol** is Professor and Chair of the Department of Puerto Rican Studies, Brooklyn College, City University of New York, Brooklyn, N.Y. **Dr. José Oscar Alers** is retired and was formerly Professor in the Dept. of Black and Hispanic Studies, Baruch College, City University of New York.

been punctuated by the *va y ven* (back-and-forth) migratory movement of many Puerto Ricans. Often propelled by economic pressures, the *va y ven* phenomenon reinforces many links to the island, although it also reflects repeated ruptures and renewals of ties, dismantlings and reconstructions of familial and communal networks in old and new settings. The economic development of Puerto Rico under U.S. domination generated a surplus population that migrated to the U.S. In effect, the creation of Puerto Rican communities in the U.S. is a direct result of the migratory flows caused by the system of production in Puerto Rico and the U.S.

At present, fully 40 percent of all Puerto Ricans live in the U.S. That is, two of every five Puerto Ricans no longer live in Puerto Rico. It is this condition that has been referred to as the "Puerto Rican diaspora" (López and Petras, 1974: 316-346), or as "the Divided Nation" (Wagenheim and Jiménez de Wagenheim, 1973: 283ff.). But there is an additional dimension to the diaspora or division: the dispersion of Puerto Ricans within the U.S. In 1940, 90 percent of all Puerto Ricans in the U.S. resided in New York City; by 1970, only 57 percent lived there. Indeed, in 1970 more than 30 U.S. cities had Puerto Rican communities of over 5,000 (U.S. Commission on Civil Rights, 1976: 21). This dispersion raises serious questions of struggle and survival for the Puerto Rican community. The papers included in this collection attempt to present varying perspectives on survival and to detail the struggles of diverse Puerto Ricans in the U.S., especially in New York City, where most of them are still concentrated.

Nature of the Collection

We feel it is important to retain the variety of style and approach of the individual papers in the collection — which reflects, to an extent, the diversity of our community. This collection does not present an analysis of all the issues relevant to the Puerto Rican experience in the U.S. There are, for example, voids on migration, education, health, and comparative research on the various communities. But what we have included within the scope of this monograph is a beginning. We hope the present collection will emphasize that there is a need to analyze and synthesize the evidence of social research, whether this be in the form of personal accounts or collec-

2

tive facts and figures. We feel that this is necessary in order to arrive at, or speak to, the new reality of Puerto Ricans, their future and a more accurate past than has been depicted in the literature thus far. This reality is described not only in the detached language of the social scientist, but in the passionate words of the participants.

Our agenda originates in a desire to tell the story, with an insider's interpretation, of Puerto Ricans struggling to survive. Not that one has to be Puerto Rican to write accurately about the Puerto Rican community, or that being Puerto Rican is any guarantee of accuracy or insight. Nevertheless, the experience of being Puerto Rican, if understood correctly, can enhance one's work. Thus, it is no accident that nearly all involved with this collection are second-generation Puerto Ricans or have otherwise experienced life in U.S. Puerto Rican communities. Although from a variety of disciplines, the authors have been intimately involved in the issues they address and this sets their work apart from many traditional social scientists.

For example, Guzmán and Fuentes have been principal actors in the political struggles they discuss. Stevens-Arroyo, as a Puerto Rican priest, is active in the Catholic Church's Hispanic programs. Rosa Estades was actively involved over a long period in the Puerto Rican Day Parade. Franklyn Sánchez and Max Salazár have long been associated with the world and activities of spiritualism and Latin music, respectively. Rosemary Santana Cooney, Alice Colón, Dale Nelson, Virginia Sánchez, José Oscar Alers, Clara Rodríguez and José Hernández have all written extensively on the Puerto Rican community, and have in many cases been actively involved in organizing and developing programs and projects in the community.

All contributors to this collection have participated in the Puerto Rican experience in the U.S. — either personally or academically or both — enough to understand a point recently made by Olga Jiménez de Wagenheim (1978), historian and author, when she spoke about the situation of Puerto Ricans in the U.S. She described Puerto Ricans as ". . . a people forever travelling between two realities, two cultures, two worlds," a people who found ". . . their strength and spiritual power in Puerto Rico, just as the smallest branch of a tree derives its strength from its roots." But the second-generation Puerto Rican has come to accept, in addition, the reality of life in the U.S. Acceptance of that reality does not mean approval or unreserved adoption of that reality. Although the branches and the trunk

3

share common roots, the view from the branches is different from the view one has from the trunk.

And even the smallest branches—as long as they are connected to their roots—have no desire to be grafted onto another trunk, even though that trunk may be called progress. For we must create our own definition of progress—a task begun by Pablo "Yoruba" Guzmán (1977), a second-generation Puerto Rican raised in one of the nation's numerous *barrios*:

> Progress is not hearing the Parkay margarine say *"mantequilla!,"* nor is it buttoned-down Latin (hyphen) Americans entering corporate madness in greater numbers; I'd much rather see us gather our forces to make this *país* less uptight and more funky, as seen in our healthier attitude towards sex, better acceptance of music, familiarity with the spirits, a greater respect for young and old, and a stronger sense of family and community. Now if we could bring some of that across, *that* would be progress.

Perspectives on Survival

The survival of a modern people is highly dependent on its written history and literature. Statistical indicators are one method of recording the history and development of a group. When these measures are not under the control of the group being measured, but are instead in the hands of researchers limited in their knowledge of those under scrutiny, they run the risk of distortion. At issue, then, is whether or not Puerto Ricans have been accurately identified and studied, and whether social-science research has produced a valid and reliable picture of the community.

In his paper for this collection, sociologist José Hernández examines the conceptual models and methods used to gather basic social-science data on Puerto Ricans. He presents an insider's view of the problems associated with "measuring" the quality of life among Puerto Ricans, and the difficulties of following a career as a Puerto Rican social scientist. Hence, this collection begins by confronting efforts which have produced prevailing interpretations of the Puerto Rican situation and by delineating the struggles within which the group had to persevere in the professional environment of the social sciences.

The Clara E. Rodríguez article on race supports the Hernández

4

viewpoint and provides essentially a twofold example. It demonstrates one aspect of the Puerto Rican experience which has often been misinterpreted by non-Latinos and bears witness to the survival of Puerto Ricans· as an identifiable racial/ethnic group. The racial factor is perhaps the greatest single deterrence to the complete assimilation of any group. Yet it is for many individual Puerto Ricans the most significant variable determining their own paths of assimilation and socialization. Thus, color, a silent but negative issue for Puerto Ricans in the island, may become in some intangible way the tie that binds Puerto Ricans in the United States, that enables the Puerto Rican community to survive as a separate entity. Focusing on how Puerto Ricans view themselves racially and how they, in turn, are viewed by non-Puerto Ricans, the essay raises the question of how Latino racial attitudes or perceptions will affect future residency and social patterns.

Until recently the insistence that Puerto Ricans were but another group in the North American assimilation process had dominated the social-science literature. But the Puerto Rican experience in the United States has undergone unique changes which have further "peculiarized" that migration and its resultant community. The time context within which most Puerto Ricans arrived and grew to maturity was a socially-sensitive period. The civil rights movement, the black revolution in esthetics, in the arts, and in the everyday facets of ghetto life strongly affected the Puerto Rican community. Challenges raised by alienated but affluent North American youth seriously questioned the traditional success-oriented goals of this society. The strong spectre of drugs in the Puerto Rican neighborhoods and the (at first) expanding welfare sector, combined with extreme economic contraction in the New York metropolitan region, influenced the nature and style of the hustle to survive in the Puerto Rican ghettos. All of these factors bore directly on a people already somewhat disinclined to assimilate into the mainstream.

The Economic Context

Puerto Ricans were very much outside of the mainstream yet very much in the middle of changing streams. Sharing neighborhoods, schools, courts, welfare centers and other city services with blacks, as well as a frail economic foothold at the bottom of the labor queue, Puerto Ricans observed at an uncomfortably close range the defiance of a system structured against them. In "Economic Survival in New York City," Clara E. Rodríguez, reflecting this growing cynicism, presents a critical examination of the structure of the New York City economy when Puerto Ricans arrived in greatest numbers. The paper investigates the position of Puerto Ricans at the bottom rung of the occupational ladder. But it differs from other occupational analyses by examining factors outside of the Puerto Rican psyche (e.g., predilection for work, or cultural attitudes). The essay transcends the generally simplistic explanations offered for the participation of Puerto Ricans as a blue-collar work force and examines instead the external structural factors impacting upon the community — the suburbanization of many jobs, the decline of manufacturing jobs in New York City, and the growth of service work.

Yet the reality of these economic forces exists ultimately in the effect they have on people's lives. Virginia Sánchez Korrol has recorded the stories of a vital part of the Puerto Rican population — Puerto Rican women. The role of Puerto Rican women both in and out of the work force has been a major one in the development and continuity of the community. Women acted as facilitators between the earlier migrants and the unfamiliar environment and as transmitters of Puerto Rican customs or traditions. Participating in the labor force was considered a natural extension of female responsibilities, since women in Puerto Rico as early as the 1920's comprised a significant percentage of the island's work force. This concept of women working in-house and out-of-the-house was brought to the New York *colonias* as part of the migrant's cultural background. "Survival of Puerto Rican Women in New York Before World War II" offers a historical glimpse into the work role of Puerto Rican women. Based on a collection of oral histories, as well as census documentation, the Puerto Rican struggle to survive during the early period is captured in the stories of the women interviewed. These stories reveal the groundwork that was laid for the resiliency of the post-war community.

A broader and more statistical picture of the labor-market experiences of the daughters, sisters, aunts and mothers of these same women is presented in "Work and Family: The Recent Struggle of Puerto Rican Females," by Rosemary Santana Cooney and Alice Colón. It contains a quantitative analysis of Puerto Rican women's participation in the labor market compared to other minority groups over two decades. An important statistical finding in the 1970 census was the stark decrease in the labor-force participation rate of Puerto Rican females since 1950. This decline is counter to what is a very significant trend among women in general, whose employment options are currently increasing in the market place. This suggests that low-skill job displacement, associated with the changing industrial structure, has severely impacted upon the working Puerto Rican female.

Cultural, Political and Spiritual Struggles

The economy and the labor market forced Puerto Ricans to migrate and limited their role in U.S. society and how well they lived. Occupational mobility and economic vitality were capped by forces hard to understand and seemingly too distant to fight. But the economic hard times merely intensified the struggles to survive in other dimensions. For example, Puerto Ricans affirmed themselves and their culture through their music, as shown by Max Salazár in his paper. The sixties, in particular, brought strong pressure to retain, affirm, perhaps perpetuate and eventually perfect being Puerto Rican.

Latin music was and is a vehicle for cultural survival, affirming a Puerto Rican identity where songs expressed the attitudes, sorrows and dreams of working people. Later, bilingual education, Puerto Rican studies, Puerto Rican flag labels and stickers, the Puerto Rican Day Parade, Latin *salsa* and the Latin hustle, all became manifestations of this affirmation. Latin music acts as a vehicle for identity clarification, much like the Spanish language. But it goes one step beyond language. Its public nature makes music a fountainhead of the Puerto Rican culture. Since the earliest days of the migration, the psychic currents of the Puerto Rican community have been conveyed through its music. Nonetheless, it remains unacknowledged and has not been fully integrated into the larger music world. In spite of its tremendous financial and cultural influence in the industry,[1] until very recently there was no "Grammy" award for the best Latin record of the year, few feature articles ever appear on Latin musicians and Latin records are almost never aired on the non-Hispanic radio stations.

A similar situation surrounds the Puerto Rican Day Parade. Perhaps the most highly-attended parade of any group in New York City, with estimates of over 500,000 Hispanics in attendance every year, it is also the parade with the least news coverage. For Puerto Ricans, the parade represents a day of cultural affirmation, a celebration of symbolic unity. Rosa Estades, a sociologist long recognized for her community participation, focuses in her paper on the historical and political factors surrounding the inception and subsequent development of the parade. The patterns described reflect the growth of the Latin community in general. The parade thus emerges as a microcosm for the political and historical currents which have affected the settlements.

Yet the cultural vibrancy, political activity and organizational abilities reflected in the Puerto Rican Day Parade and in Latin music have seldom surfaced in electoral activities. It is an enigma to observers of the Puerto Rican community that a people with such high levels of political participation in Puerto Rico (as demonstrated in registration and voting figures) show such low turn-outs in U.S. elections. Dale Nelson explores statistically the relationship between assimilation, acculturation and political behavior among Puerto Ricans in New York City. He shows that the expectations that flow from the assimilation model for Puerto Ricans are not borne out in his empirical data on Puerto Ricans. Politically, then, Puerto Ricans have not followed the patterns expected by assimilation theorists. According to the data, Puerto Ricans have not assimilated politically to the U.S. mold.

But if the political intensity of Puerto Ricans has not shown up in their voting behavior, it has become front-page and even nation-wide news in other forms. Luis Fuentes and Pablo "Yoruba" Guzmán recount their personal involvement in two well-known political battles. "The Struggle for Local Political Control" describes a painfully frustrating attempt to gain community school-board control by a Puerto Rican and multi-ethnic community coalition who sought to protect their ethnic community by controlling their children's education. The creation of the Young Lords, on the other hand, along with the Puerto Rican Socialist Party, the Puerto Rican Revolutionary Workers' Organization, the Puerto Rican Student Union, El Comité and others demonstrate the political struggle to survive as Puerto Ricans in the barrios of an ethnically repressive and politically powerful society.

8

Puerto Ricans exist neither by bread, nor music, nor politics alone. Puerto Ricans are also a spiritual people, and here too the struggles have been intense. The survival of the Puerto Rican spirit is discussed from two totally different perspectives. Antonio Stevens-Arroyo writes of the attempts made by the Catholic Church to meet the spiritual and material needs of the Puerto Rican community. Experienced with the problems of immigrant groups, the Church had historically sponsored ethnic or national parishes where religious services, national customs and native languages were preserved. But after the influx of European immigrants and at the time of the greatest Puerto Rican migratory movements, the Church, under new leadership, endorsed different methods of delivering pastoral services. The ultimate outcome of these measures was to encourage the alienation of many Puerto Ricans from the Catholic Church. It is this issue that forms the focus of Antonio Stevens-Arroyo's "Puerto Rican Struggles in the Catholic Church."

Organized religion is only a part of the spiritual life of Puerto Ricans. It has long been recognized that spiritualism plays an important positive role in the mental health of the Puerto Rican community (Rogler and Hollingshead, 1961). The relationship of spiritualism or spiritism to the psychic survival of the community is significant, for it provides a continuous and socially-sanctioned means for struggling against the mental abuse of economic and social oppression. An increasing number of Puerto Rican and non-Puerto Rican health professionals have argued for better coordination between established health services and spiritualist centers in the treatment of mental illness. Franklyn D. Sánchez illustrates the similarities and differences in both modalities.

NOTE

1. A recent New York Times article ("The beat that is Latinizing disco and pop," 7/8/79, pp. 1D and 21D) quotes a conservative estimate of $25 million per year in domestic record sales.

REFERENCES

Guzmán, Pablo "Yoruba." "Which road to progress?" Nuestro 1 (5):38. 1977.

López, Adalberto and James Petras, eds. Puerto Rico and Puerto Ricans. Cambridge, Mass.: Schenkman. 1974.

Rogler, Lloyd and A.B. Hollingshead. "The Puerto Rican spiritualist as a psychiatrist." American Journal of Sociology 67(1): 17-21. 1961.

U.S. Commission on Civil Rights. Puerto Ricans in the Continental United States: An Uncertain Future. Washington, D.C.: U.S. Commission on Civil Rights, October. 1976.

Wagenheim, Kal and Olga Jiménez de Wagenheim. The Puerto Ricans: A Documentary History. New York: Praeger. 1973.

Wagenheim, Olga Jiménez de. "On Being Puerto Rican in the U.S." Paper presented to the Hispanic students at Rutgers University, Newark, New Jersey. 1978.

Social Science and the Puerto Rican Community

Introduction

It is significant that the first article in this collection was a critique of the scholarship on Puerto Ricans, for much of the subsequent work in the field of Puerto Rican Studies has taken a critical view of earlier work. Those Puerto Ricans who approached the early literature on the Puerto Rican experience felt a strong discomfort with the work they encountered because they felt the work did not reflect what they had experienced as Puerto Ricans. In the words of a recent doctoral student: "He did not find himself there." Although critiques of the literature had been vocalized often enough at meetings, conferences and other forums—in both the English and Spanish languages—little had been written in English that was critical of the work on Puerto Ricans. Some criticisms were found inserted in various doctoral works, but Hernández' article was the first to address the issue frontally and to examine some of the basic precepts used to research Puerto Ricans.

The article was also the first to make points that subsequently came to be researched and acknowledged as facts. For example, it noted that Puerto Ricans had been "researched by social scientists, mostly by experts who are neither Puerto Rican nor closely related to the community." Indeed, there is a preponderance of work written by non–Puerto Ricans in the early literature: of the 20 most significant English-language books on Puerto Ricans produced prior to 1972, only one was authored by a Puerto Rican. Although there were English-language works produced by Puerto Ricans on Puerto Ricans prior to 1973 (e.g., Fernández Mendez, 1972; Seda Bonilla, 1973), they were few in number and with scant exceptions (e.g., Padilla, 1958) did not receive the same academic attention.

The article also articulates the need for valid and reliable theories that would more accurately depict Puerto Ricans. As a trained demographer, Hernández applied his skills to examine the problems of social science models and the methods used to study Puerto Ricans. He also pointed out how the conclusions of these models often differed from the experiences of most Puerto Ricans. Underlying his article was a very basic question: that was whether social science research models—as they were currently employed and articulated—were adequate vehicles by which to study the Puerto Rican experience. The article suggested that perhaps the "white man" was not the best standard by which to measure the success or failures of Puerto Ricans. This is a question that has been central to the study of other groups as well, for instance, women, Native American Indians, etc.

Two other important contributions of the article were that it drew attention to (1) the dire need to develop more social scientists and (2) the factors accounting for the current lack of Puerto Rican social scientists. Hernández made clear, as perhaps few have done since, that it was also a struggle for Puerto Ricans to survive as academicians in the social sciences. Furthermore, he proposed that there was a need to open up organizational opportunities and to develop cooperative, indigenous ventures such as that exemplified by the papers in this volume.

Placed in its historical context, the Hernández article is an early reflection of the more extensive critical analysis and probing that was to become ascendant in the period to follow. (See bibliography in this volume and Rodríguez, 1995.) This basic questioning, and examining of issues that were heretofore unresearched or unquestioned, was begun by Puerto Ricans and others in Ethnic Studies. It would come to be echoed (but often not quoted or acknowledged) in more traditional academic departments by deconstructionists and post modernists (Vázquez, 1992).

SOCIAL SCIENCE AND
THE PUERTO RICAN COMMUNITY

by José Hernández

Social-science research on Puerto Ricans has a long history that we cannot review in detail in this paper. The story goes back many years in the experience of a colonized society and more recently involves the extension to Puerto Rico of the American social-science establishment. Continental Puerto Ricans have also been researched by social scientists, mostly by experts who are neither Puerto Rican nor closely related to the community. Very few would argue against the idea that a social science by Puerto Ricans and for the community has yet to become a realistic development.

In working toward this goal, we must somehow reconcile the requirements of social science with the notions and practical concerns that Puerto Ricans in and out of the community propose for consideration. Basically, the combination should include: (a) the creation of appropriate concepts and explanatory models, (b) the application of research methods producing valid and reliable information, and (c) the conduct of activities that enhance professional capabilities and the communication of knowledge. The three aspects to be discussed refer to issues commonly found in anthropology, economics, history, political science, psychology, sociology, and such related fields as counseling, demography, linguistics, and urban or ethnic studies.

Explanatory Models

Just as the theory of evolution in life and the notion of an atom help to understand natural reality, the social sciences use concepts

Dr. José Hernández is Professor of Sociology, Department of Black and Puerto Rican Studies, Hunter College, City University of New York, New York, N.Y.

like labor supply and demand, and general explanations for the ways in which people learn to act as they mature. The natural and social sciences share the goal of advancing only those concepts and models that consistently accord with factual evidence. Not just anybody's ideas become "valid and reliable." They must be tested and discussed, retested and discussed again. Typically, the major effort is directed to measure a concept like social class and to prove or disprove declarative statements—for example, that social class results from ownership of the means of economic production.

The quest for valid and reliable theories has led to the establishment of traditional lines of thought in the social sciences. As successful concepts and models arose, they motivated efforts by other scholars and gave shape to the questions asked. Today we are still concerned with power and authority, many years after the distinction was made among "traditional, legal-rational, and charismatic" styles of leadership. These basic explanations and subsequent refinements have generally relied on the type of information and environment that originally influenced a certain set of ideas. In many cases the principal reference is to elements of the European experience such as the French Revolution and to European thinkers like Charles Darwin, Sigmund Freud, Karl Marx, Jean Piaget, Adam Smith, Arnold Toynbee, and Max Weber.

The expectation is that new social-science work—even regarding people not European in background—will somehow conform with traditional concepts and models. For example, migration from rural Puerto Rico to New York City can be said to illustrate movement from a traditional *Gemeinschaft* to a modern *Gesellschaft* society. In so defining it, Puerto Rican migration is likened to the urbanization of the Central European peasant and the voluminous literature on the topic of industrialization, initiated in response to the condition of factory workers in the European cities of a hundred years ago.

Undoubtedly some resemblance exists and certain insights can be gained by such comparisons. The *Gemeinschaft/Gesellschaft* model is, however, only partially valid and reliable as an explanation of the Puerto Rican experience. For example, it says little or nothing about the reverse movement of people from the formality and impersonality of the modern cosmopolitan scene to the socially close and less structured environment of traditional society, which has taken place in return migration to Puerto Rico. Nor does it help to understand the situation of Puerto Ricans in a *post*industrial society like New York City, where most of the available jobs are in human services, instead of a factory, or not available at all, for such reasons as the displacement of workers by machines. Again, the basic notion of the changes involved is contradicted by evidence showing that certain aspects of the Puerto Rican lifestyle remain the same or have been actually revitalized in the United States experience.

Reliance on American social science may provide an alternative to European concepts and models. Generally, the topics more closely relate to the Puerto Rican experience because they concern the society Puerto Ricans confront in the struggle for survival. But most explanations remain partial in that attention centers on American society, with little or no consideration for marginally-situated groups. For example, analysis of the cultural origins of behavioral patterns supports the view of the United States as a "melting pot," to which newly-added groups contribute and eventually assimilate — losing their previous ethnic identity and lifestyle in the Americanization process. While this explains certain elements of change among continental Puerto Ricans, most of the evidence points to the continued affirmation of a Puerto Rican identity and a desire to preserve a lifestyle really different from that of the average person in the United States.

Another example in which the Puerto Rican experience differs from standard explanations are the social "stratification" categories (e.g., upper-middle, middle, lower-middle, upper-lower) that have been extensively researched. Although these distinctions say much about class differences among the American majority, they are of limited use regarding Puerto Ricans. Puerto Ricans typically remain outside the usual American class structure, in that neither the usual symbols of status (language, possessions, place of residence, etc.) nor the behavior associated with these categories are commonly found. Instead, certain class situations generally ignored by the social sciences are more descriptive. For example, in cities where the Puerto Rican community is relatively small, it is typically located at the fringe of the black ghetto, in strips politely called a "buffer zone," which supposes some mediating or insulating function. The reality often involves a precarious life of substandard housing, scarce or unavailable public services, and little or no access to such means of social mobility as jobs, specialized training, or participation in voluntary associations and programs.

Discrimination against Puerto Ricans makes difficult whatever improvement may be possible in their marginal economic situation. To be hired for the same job and earn the same money as a white non-Puerto Rican, a Puerto Rican must generally have more education and experience. In fact, the average income of a Puerto Rican college graduate is about equal to that of a white non-Puerto Rican high school graduate of the same age.[1] A similar wage difference is true of blacks, and of white women, compared with white men. But most social scientists who study the way Puerto Ricans live agree that the similarity of experience with blacks and white women is limited to the most essential aspects of being disadvantaged in American society. For Puerto Ricans, discrimination is not as widely recognized to exist, and exactly how people are excluded from job, promotion and earning opportunities has not been studied in detail.

Until detailed research has been completed on the topic, a "minority" model based on other people's experience will have limited explanatory value for Puerto Ricans. We need to know, for example, how important physical appearance is in prejudice, how cultural factors such as language, a person's manner of dress or name contribute to discrimination. Much more knowledge is necessary regarding situational aspects: having a certain address, or listing Puerto Rico as one's birthplace, and many other factors that remain to be determined. Stated as briefly as possible, a social science with concepts fully appropriate and applicable to Puerto Ricans has yet to be developed.

Research Methods

The traditional ways to develop social science have been by conducting surveys and experiments, or from information collected by observation and case histories, or the use of available materials from libraries and similar sources. Each of these avenues to acquire knowledge has a set of professional guidelines called "methodology" which governs the way research is conducted. As in the case of explanatory models, an important question to consider is how appropriate and applicable social-science methods are for Puerto Ricans.

Among the methods just mentioned, the survey is the most

frequently chosen by agencies seeking data about Puerto Ricans. The survey's popularity stems partly from the prestige it has acquired in public-opinion polls, the Census, and the related gathering of information that contributes directly to policy-making in government. The survey also has several advantages, principally the convenience of standard questions, application by telephone or postal service, and easy processing of results by computer. However, the survey is by far the most expensive social-science method, and it requires laboratories and time-consuming preparations, if anything different from conventional practices is attempted. Also, collecting information by questionnaire constrains people to respond as individuals and, generally speaking, in a manner predetermined by the researcher.

A few special surveys have produced much of what is known about Puerto Ricans in the social-science literature. Yet these studies have raised more questions than they have answered, because the traditional methods of collecting the data have omitted or only partially covered many matters particular to the Puerto Rican experience. These surveys were also limited to singular efforts, without a chance to return and gather more adequate information. Only recently has information been produced by surveys that are repeated on a regular basis, but in these cases the subject matter is very limited. For many years people were not routinely identified as Puerto Rican, and now that self-designation is becoming a standard item on forms and questionnaires, Puerto Ricans make up only a small fragment of the individuals randomly sampled throughout the United States. With so few cases and with questions designed for the broad spectrum of the American public, only limited results have become available for Puerto Ricans.

As the resources for social research diminished in the 1970's, researchers turned to methods other than the survey. The experiment, for example, has attracted greater attention, especially as applied to human situations of everyday concern. Studies testing for discrimination in housing have compared the results of applications or complaints by minority persons with those submitted by majority persons — for the same rental, loan or insurance policy, or for the same adverse condition. Such experiments provide convincing evidence because of the scientific nature of the method, which enables a researcher to relate a factor like minority status to housing availability in a simple, direct manner. The experiment can usually

17

be repeated and readily compared with results in different circumstances. Whether the results obtained in a few trials represent all or most situations is an issue requiring special attention in any experiment. In addition, certain problems may distort the information, as happens when the people involved suspect that they are being studied. Not much can be said about the experiment among Puerto Ricans, because little social-science research has used this method with them as subjects.

The observation and case-history method is somewhat different, in that several studies have relied on the account of a researcher who has visited or lived in a Puerto Rican community and recorded information on social topics. The results are typically presented in a book that portrays the Puerto Rican people at a certain time and in ways considered most important by the observer. Like the experiment, the observation and case-history method is relatively inexpensive, direct, and simple. When properly done, it enables the community to speak for itself in full detail, providing the most flexibility for learning about things uniquely Puerto Rican. But compared with other methods, this approach has a greater tendency to produce results influenced by the researcher's opinions, instead of factual information. Another problem can occur in reducing the many particular items of information that even a short period of observation may yield to a set of brief conclusions about the community in general.

Use of available data sources is a promising approach to research about Puerto Ricans, if the information exists and is accurate. It is generally the cheapest method and often the most readily activated and effective in completing a limited social-science research project. Organizations routinely gather facts about people who are members, clients, or in some way involved in their activities. For example, school records can provide important data for the study of the success or failure of Puerto Ricans in the educational system. As in many surveys, the nature of the information, and the format in which it is recorded, may be standardized and overlook major aspects of the Puerto Rican experience, especially in such areas as motivation, discouragement, and other human feelings. Access to available data may also be limited by regulations meant to safeguard people's right to privacy and their confidence when furnishing personal information.

From the discussion so far, we can conclude that no method is ideal and that each remains to be adequately adapted and applied to

Puerto Ricans. The best approach would combine the strengths of two or more methods in a comprehensive study of a major policy topic like discrimination. But almost any project using appropriate methods to study a worthwhile aspect of the social life of Puerto Ricans would contribute important knowledge. What is really needed are motivated people who will carry an idea to completion with the energy and honesty demanded for good social-science research.

Professional Activities

Perhaps the greatest limitation in developing social science for Puerto Ricans is the lack of human resources in the field. Among continental Puerto Ricans there are only some twenty fully-credentialed social scientists, a fraction of the number necessary to make a difference in research and the dissemination of knowledge. Moreover, much of this scarce talent is now engaged in other activities, such as administration, teaching, consultation, and committee work. Although graduate students currently finishing advanced degrees will expand the number of workers, even this addition will be small and most will not be concerned primarily with research. The outlook for the formation and growth of an indigenous group of professional researchers is therefore disappointing.

To some extent, the same factors affecting job opportunities for the average Puerto Rican are also operative in the social sciences. Few Puerto Ricans are eligible for higher education, because of the high push-out rate among secondary-school students. Those who graduate from high school and go on to college are often discouraged from seeking a career in the social sciences either because these disciplines lack a clear connection with their human experience and what Puerto Ricans know about the community, or because they do not see it as a realistic goal. To occupy a professional position in the social sciences, an effort and investment comparable to medical school is necessary. This entails several years beyond a college degree to become firmly established in a job and recognized in the profession. For persons facing disadvantages and deprivations compared with affluent Americans, the length of time and sacrifice involved does not always make sense.

In a profession that pioneered the study of inequality in United

States society it is ironic that Puerto Ricans who follow a social-science career should face discrimination in practice. Although the factual evidence has not been fully assembled, experience shows that entry and success are not easily attained, nor attainable on equal terms with other students. Puerto Rican college students are typically given minimal or no participation in social-research activities that might help develop skills appropriate to the profession. Graduate students are often delayed in scholarly advancement by the need to learn a large body of knowledge unrelated to the Puerto Rican experience, receiving virtually no instruction of relevance or directly applicable to the Puerto Rican community. Newly-graduated social scientists must accumulate publications in traditional journals to strengthen their standing and gain a continuing position at a university.

For the mature Puerto Rican social scientist, the usual situation is an overload of professional duties like serving on advisory and review boards, with only meager resources for original research. As an example of how funds are allocated, one of the largest federal investments in social research relative to Puerto Ricans was a National Institute of Child Health and Human Development contract for research on the education, employment, marriage and childbearing patterns of Hispanic women. Awarded in 1972 to a majority male researcher, this project produced a paper in 1975 which admonished Puerto Rican women to improve their low schooling and job status by seeking advanced training, white-collar work, marriage to majority husbands, and small families as a success formula for middle-class status. However, the outlook was said to be gloomy for Puerto Ricans, because "significant educational differentials will continue . . . for at least several decades into the future." On the basis of these differentials, it appears that the researchers who perform such studies will not be Puerto Ricans for several decades into the future, either.

In summary, the social sciences involve as much a struggle to survive as other aspects of social life for Puerto Ricans in the United States. The issues and examples discussed show the variability of research results, depending on how Puerto Ricans are viewed as participants in the American social system and the ways in which their social life is studied. The profession remains dominated by non-Puerto Rican scholars and by traditional norms and procedures that seldom generate an excellent or even adequate portrayal of our social reality. A redirection of explanatory models and methods in response and adaptation to Puerto Ricans therefore becomes a major goal. Professional involvement and advancement of Puerto Ricans in the social sciences represents a key element for change, if their participation is to be genuinely effective. A realistic strategy for basic social-science reform begins with the opening of organizational opportunities, but places the main emphasis on the kind of cooperative, indigenous venture exemplified by the papers in this collection.

NOTE

1. Evidence for this difference is presented in José Hernández (1979) and U.S. Commission on Civil Rights (1978).

REFERENCES

Hernández, José. "Hispanic Migration and Demographic Patterns: Implications for Educational Planning and Policy." ERIC Clearinghouse on Urban Education. New York: Columbia University Teachers College. 1979.
U.S. Commission on Civil Rights. Social Indicators of Equality for Minorities and Women. Washington, D.C.: U.S. Commission on Civil Rights. 1978.

Puerto Ricans:
Between Black and White

Introduction

Puerto Ricans entered the northeastern part of the United States in substantial numbers after a long immigration hiatus. They entered a world that was composed of relatively assimilated (2nd and 3rd generation) Euro-Americans and African-American migrants from the South. As the largest multiracial migration to the northeast, they were the first to experience what subsequent multiracial immigrant groups would also experience. In the racial realm, these were pressures to identify as a color instead of as a culture, a "browning" process, perceptual dissonance, and challenges to different constructions of "race." Subsequent groups would come with somewhat different racial mixtures, e.g., a greater mix of Amerindian heritages. Moreover, they would experience challenges to racial constructions in contexts that had been more internationalized—because of the large numbers of immigrants entering the country from many countries. Thus, nativist fears might be more articulated, but so were their opponents.

As with many of the articles in this collection, by describing the situation then, the article continued to spur interest in this area on the part of other scholars (see, for example, Martínez, 1988). In addition, the basic issue it addresses of racial classification has also become a very important issue for the U.S. government. Because of the "dilemma" that increasing numbers of multiracial peoples present to the biracial structure of the United States, the government is currently considering proposals to alter the way in which the race question is asked. One of the proposals receiving serious attention is the proposal to make Hispanics a race. Millions of dollars are being spent on researching the impact of such a change on the year 2000 census. (U.S. Department of Commerce, 1995b.) Tens of thousands of households are being interviewed to determine whether they should be asked either (a) two questions, i.e., one about their "race," and the other about whether they are of Hispanic origin; or (b) one question, which would be a "race" question that would have "Hispanic" included as one of the categories (U.S. Office of Management and Budget, 1995; U.S. Dept. of Labor, 1995a).

Whatever the outcome of these studies, the issues that were outlined in this article in 1974 are at the core of these considerations. The enduring timeliness of these issues is reflected in the fact that the article was recently reprinted in 1995, as part of a collection of influential writings on Boricuas (Puerto Ricans) by Santiago (1995).

PUERTO RICANS:
BETWEEN BLACK AND WHITE

by Clara E. Rodríguez

The experience of Puerto Ricans in New York City points up more clearly than any researched materials the chasm that exists between whites and blacks in the United States and the racism that afflicts both groups. For within the U.S. perspective, Puerto Ricans, racially speaking, belong to both groups; however, ethnically, they belong to neither. Thus placed, Puerto Ricans find themselves caught between two polarities and at a dialectical distance from both. Puerto Ricans are between white and black; Puerto Ricans are neither white nor black.

To understand the apparent contradictions in these statements, it is necessary to understand the racial history of Puerto Ricans and the present-day social correlates of this history, the racial experience of Puerto Ricans arriving in New York, and the reactions of New York Puerto Ricans to the dialectical reality of which they are a part, and a result.

Racial History and Contrasts

The degree to which racial heterogeneity is an integral factor of Puerto Rican life must be appreciated. It is not just a matter of black and white families within a community; it is more often a matter of a Negro-appearing brother and his Anglo-appearing sister attending the same school. The variety of racial types in the Puerto Rican community is the biological result of a still-not-clearly-analyzed his-

Dr. Clara E. Rodríguez is Professor of Sociology, Fordham College at Lincoln Center, New York, N.Y. This paper is reprinted by permission of New York Affairs. Copyright 1974 by Urban Periodicals, Inc.

tory of racial mixing. Although a number of works have touched upon the issue of racial mixing in Puerto Rico, there is no real consensus in this area. Puerto Rican and American researchers have assumed or found Puerto Rico to be everything from a mulatto country to a predominantly white country with small subgroups of blacks and mulattos. Nevertheless, the process of racial mixing has continued and the existence of significant racial heterogeneity continues.

This same history has also yielded a unique set of social attitudes which have created a racial ambience quite different from that in the U.S. This ambience is vital to the understanding of the Puerto Rican experience in New York. A few of these points of contrast might bring about a better understanding of the racial ambience from which Puerto Ricans come and hence the racial attitudes that accompany racially heterogeneous Puerto Ricans to New York.

Perhaps the primary point of contrast is that, in Puerto Rico, racial identification is subordinate to cultural identification, while in the U.S., racial identification, to a large extent, determines cultural identification. Thus when asked that divisive question, "What are you?" Puerto Ricans of all colors and ancestry answer, "Puerto Rican," while most New Yorkers answer, black, Jewish, or perhaps, "of Italian descent." This is not to say that Puerto Ricans feel no racial identification, but rather that cultural identification supercedes it.

Analyzing the system of racial classification in Puerto Rico we see that it is based more on phenotypic and social definitions of what a person is than on genotypic knowledge about a person. In other words, physical and social appearance are the measures used to classify instead of the biological-descent classification (i.e., "one drop of Negro blood makes you Negro") used in the U.S. Thus in the U.S. the white-appearing offspring of an interracial couple is classified "Negro."[1] In Puerto Rico, he would probably be white. Alternatively, an obviously dark or "colored" person in the U.S. may not be seen as dark in Puerto Rico, especially if there are other mitigating circumstances, class for example. Many other examples of the contrasting racial classification criteria could be cited, but these two serve to point up the main differences.[2]

Another aspect of racial classification in Puerto Rico is that racial categories are based on color, class, facial features and texture of hair. This is quite in contrast to the mainly color-based, white-nonwhite, or white, black, yellow, red and brown classifications of the U.S. This makes for a spectrum of racial types in Puerto Rico. There are *blancos*, the equivalent of whites in this country;³ *indios* are similar to the U.S. conception of East Indians, i.e., dark-skinned and straight-haired; *morenos* are dark-skinned, with a variety of features, Negroid and Caucasian; *negros* are the black, Black men in the U.S. (As an aside, it is interesting that this latter term is also used as a term of endearment, at which time it bears no connotation of color whatsoever and can be used to refer to any of the racial types.) It can also, however, be used, depending on the tone, as a derogative term, like "nigger." Lastly, is the term *"trigueño"* which can be applied to what would be considered brunettes in this country or to Negroes or *negros* who have high social status. Despite this term's lack of congruity with physical characteristics, it is still considered a term of racial classification; it just goes both ways.

The fact that this term goes both ways is indicative of the relationship between class and race. A "black" or "negro" person becomes "white" by achieving economic status or one's friendship. It is an obvious form of "passing" without, however, the connotations given to that term in the U.S. In this country, a person who passes has become outwardly white. His physical appearance and cultural ways are white. In Puerto Rico a *"trigueño,"* who is Negro and moves up the status ladder, has not changed and is not furtively seeking escape from identification as a Negro.

Next there is the contrast of a biracial, multi-ethnic society versus a homogeneous society. While in the U.S. racial/ethnic minorities have traditionally been segregated, there has never been any such tradition in Puerto Rico. Thus blacks in Puerto Rico are not a distinguishable ethnic group. This is not to say blacks are evenly distributed throughout the social structure, for there is, at present, some debate on this issue. But in terms of housing, institutional treatment, political rights, government policy and cultural identification, black, white and tan Puerto Ricans are not different. And race is not perceived as an issue on the island by Puerto Ricans of any pigmentation. Perhaps the clearest testament to this situation is the lack of response of dark Puerto Ricans on the island to the black-power movement. This is in contrast to the high degree of involvement in the black movement evidenced by Puerto Ricans of all colors in New York. Thus, while dark Puerto Ricans on the island are not a distinct

27

ethnic group, Puerto Ricans of all colors in New York are.

One reflection of this unified society is that there is not the same taboo on intermarriage between white and black that exists in the U.S. Thus Puerto Ricans have intermarried and continue to intermarry at what is probably a higher frequency than the U.S. And the strong emphasis on close family ties tends to make the world of most Puerto Rican children one that is inhabited by people of many colors, and these colors are not associated with different ranks.[4] This intermingled white, black and tan world is foreign to most children in the U.S.

One-way Street

This leads us into another area of contrast: two-way integration as opposed to one-way integration. In the U.S., one-way integration has been and is the norm. That is, blacks are usually sent to white schools, not vice versa; blacks integrate into white America, not whites into black America. For example, in this country a black couple almost never adopts a white child. The number of white babies available for adoption and the limited income of many blacks tend to discourage this action. In most adoption agencies the action is not permitted and the reverse is encouraged. In Puerto Rico, it is a fairly common occurrence to rear other people's children as one's own. These *hijos de crianza* come in all colors. Thus, a "dark" couple may rear the lighter, orphaned children of a relative or neighbor and a "white" couple may be rearing their own or another's "dark" child.

Furthermore, blacks or their contributions to U.S. culture are often white-washed. Blacks in the U.S. have become more and more aware of how their cultural contributions to U.S. music, for example, have been "stolen," commercialized, denigrified. In Puerto Rico, the island music is a synthesis of Indian, African and Spanish elements and is perceived as Puerto Rican. A similar type of synthesis is evolving in the New York Puerto Rican community; the new Latin sound incorporates Afro-Cuban, white rock, black soul and the Latin rhythms. All Puerto Ricans in New York — white, black and tan — continue to dance to this new music in the same way. This is quite different from the situation that has traditionally existed in the U.S., where blacks and whites not only tend to dance differently, but to different music. Thus while jazz split into white and black, Puerto

28

Rican music development in New York and Puerto Rico was unitive. The rip-off process of whites and the indignation of blacks are possible only in a biracial, one-way society.

These descriptions of the racial climate in Puerto Rico should not be taken to imply the complete lack of discrimination in Puerto Rico. There is, at present, substantial debate over the "prejudice of no prejudice in Puerto Rico."[5] Some of the important questions currently being raised are: have Indian and African elements been destroyed or integrated into society? is the race issue in Puerto Rico dealt with by ignoring it, or is it really not an issue? do all Puerto Ricans have some African ancestry? is this condition necessary for harmonious "race" relations? is there prejudice against Africanisms in Puerto Rico? is this prejudice an American import? is there an unrecognized color gradient as one moves up the income scale? If so, is this due to Puerto Rican preferential policies for light Puerto Ricans, discriminatory policies against blacks, inequalities inherited from slavery days or the result of American imperialism? Is the whole debate over whether there is prejudice in Puerto Rico the result of a colonialized mentality?

Perceptual Dissonance

Despite the debate, the contrasts in racial climates in the U.S. and Puerto Rico exist and persist. Consequently these two climates have led to the development of widely different racial attitudes on the part of Puerto Ricans and other New Yorkers. These attitudinal differences coupled with the racial heterogeneity of Puerto Ricans have created a perceptual incongruence, with the inevitable strains accruing mainly to Puerto Ricans in New York. Given the racist perceptions in New York (and the U.S.), Puerto Ricans are not accepted by blacks or whites as a culturally distinct, racially-integrated group, but are rather perceived and consequently treated as either black or white Puerto Ricans. Racial distinctions are heightened to a degree unnatural to Puerto Ricans (although blacks may be more aware of the cultural distinctness of Puerto Ricans, they still *perceive* in American racial terms). Given their racial heterogeneity, different racial perceptions and awareness of the negative effects of racial reclassification in the U.S., Puerto Ricans generally exhibit considerable resistance to these divisive racial perceptions.

Thus there are only two options open in biracial New York — to be white or black. These options negate the cultural existence of Puerto Ricans and ignore their insistence on being treated, irrespective of race, as a culturally intact group. Thus, U.S. racial attitudes necessarily make Puerto Ricans either white or black, attitudes and culture make them neither white nor black, and our own resistance and struggle for survival places us between whites and blacks.[6]

This struggle for survival has not left Puerto Ricans unaffected. On the contrary, this in-between position has affected individual perceptions as well as group identity. Historically, Puerto Ricans arriving in New York have found themselves in a situation of perceptual incongruence — that is, they saw themselves differently than they were seen.

Some recently-gathered data attest to the persistence of this situation. Fifty-two first- and second-generation Puerto Ricans in New York were asked to classify themselves in terms of color; meanwhile, the interviewer also classified respondents in terms of color using, however, U.S. racial classifications. The U.S. racial categorizations were based on whether or not the person would be considered white by white Americans in a white setting (see Table 1). Thus, those in the first category would pass without any question. Those in the second category might pass for white but would stand out a little. Those in the third category are noticeably not white, but also are not black, e.g., Filipino and South Pacific types. And in the fourth category are those with strong traces of African ancestry.

Table 1. Racial Classification of Puerto Rican Respondents by Interviewers and by Respondents Themselves

Percent of Respondents Classified According to U.S. Categories as:		Percent of Respondents Classifying Themselves as:	
Unquestionably white	29	White, *blanco*	37
White, possibly	34	White Puerto Rican, *blanco trigueño,* beige	13
Not white, not black	32	Brown, *indio, grifo,* Indian, *moreno*	35
Black, Negro	5	Negro, mulatto, *de color,* black Puerto Rican, *prieto*	13
		Don't know	2

To the extent that the respondents were correctly classified in terms of U.S. standards, the results are intriguing. The only category in which there was no difference of opinion with respect to racial identification was the fourth. That is to say, a substantial proportion of respondents had self-perceptions of their color that differed from the U.S. perspective; however, all those with visible African ancestry perceived themselves as black. Many who were not seen as black, according to U.S. standards, saw themselves as black; hence while 13 percent of the respondents saw themselves as black the interviewer saw only five percent of the respondents as black.

On the other side of the color spectrum, more people saw themselves as "unquestionably white" than were thus classified — 37 percent compared with 29 percent. However, some who were classified "unquestionably white" saw themselves as brown or tan. This indicates a "browning" tendency on the part of these "unquestionably white" Puerto Ricans; the so-called U.S. melting pot seems to "brown" Puerto Ricans. There were none classified "unquestionably white" who saw themselves as black.

There was, on the whole, however, a very strong tendency for respondents of both generations to classify themselves as darker than perceived by the interviewer. This was most evident in the "white, possibly" category. This (as defined by U.S. standards) was the most fluctuating and largest category of respondents. It was here that a significant number perceived themselves as brown, black and Indian. However, it was also here that some perceived themselves as "unquestionably white."[7] Thus while this was the only category in which a few respondents saw themselves as lighter than they were seen, many people in this category also saw themselves as darker than they were seen.

It is possible that for these "white, possibly" Puerto Ricans, color has never been as issue. Perhaps they have not been periodically excluded from white groups or automatically included in black groups. (Nor have they been automatically included in white groups and excluded from black groups.) It is also possible that these "light" Puerto Ricans are members of a group which they think is considered non-white and so might, therefore, categorize themselves as darker. Furthermore, it is possible that they are perceived as darker than they are, when it becomes known they are Puerto Rican. Both situations would result in a darker racial self-image.

These still tentative results do indicate that there exists important perceptual dissonance between Puerto Ricans and Americans. For although not all respondents had perceptions of their color that differed from those of the U.S., most did. There was, in addition, one respondent who said he did not know what his color was — a rather unusual reply in the U.S. This was perhaps indicative of a refusal to be slotted into black-white categories.

Given the racial heterogeneity of many Puerto Rican families, it would seem that family makeup also has much to do with their racial self-perception. Often the darkest or darker *in the family* usually do see themselves as non-white and/or darker than their actual color. This tended to be true for both first- and second-generation groups.

Although this small study raises more questions than it answers, its principal conclusion is clear; Puerto Ricans see themselves very differently than they are seen by American standards.

Puerto Ricans, New Yoricans and Ricans

This perceptual incongruence points up the different mental-racial environment within which Puerto Ricans have functioned since they came to New York. Puerto Ricans living in the U.S. in the seventies have a considerably different mind set than those who were among the early migrants.

The early–migrating Puerto Ricans entered a biracial society that strictly associated white with positive and black with negative. The migrating Puerto Rican saw that this association permeated every aspect of American life. There were the "nice" neighborhoods and the Negro neighborhoods. There were the Americans and the Negroes. There were also innumerable times he learned he was being given preference over a black — while, on the other hand, finding himself accepted and treated as a black, racially or socially.

The result of this situation was that the migrant Puerto Rican held on to his cultural identity very strongly and rejected racial identification on American terms. This prompted a bitter reaction from the black community capsuled in the words, "Trouble is they (Puerto Ricans) won't call themselves colored and we won't call them white." For the migrant Puerto Rican this racial identification, and all it implied, was not only foreign to his cultural and perceptual frame of reference, it was also damning.

However, with the black renaissance and black-power movement of the sixties, there have been significant changes. These changes are more apparent in the New York-bred second generation, but they are also visible in the first generation. A new response to perceptual incongruence appears to be developing. This is exemplified in the growing acceptance of the term "non-white" to describe New York Puerto Ricans.[8] The "browning process" found in the data cited previously appears to be consistent with this development.

Seen within a dialectical framework, darker racial self–perceptions and the acceptance of a non-white categorization appear to be indicative of a nascent synthesis of two diametrically opposed perceptions of Puerto Ricans. Puerto Ricans, a culturally–homogeneous, racially-integrated group, find themselves opposed to the demand that they become racially divided and culturally "cleansed" of being Puerto Rican.

What does the term "non-white" mean? Is this a racial term? Non-white is to New York Puerto Ricans what Puerto Ricans and blacks are; "white" is what Puerto Ricans and blacks are not. However, "black" is what blacks are and Puerto Ricans are not. This increasingly common definition of Puerto Ricans as "non-white" can also be seen as an evolution of racial perceptions and classifications engendered in Puerto Rico. For the predominance of cultural over racial considerations is evident in the development of this new "racial" term, which embraces all colors and types of Puerto Ricans.

The extent to which this growing acceptance of non-white categorization and the extent to which the "browning process" has been affected by political as well as historical and cultural forces can also be seen. For many New York Puerto Ricans have come of age at a time when black consciousness was in its renaissance — when the strength of black power was evident from the frightened faces of whites. The clear messages of these movements placed the option of assimilation in a different light and, more importantly, provided the possibility and example of an alternative to white-defined identities.[9]

An increasing number of (white, black and tan) New York Puerto Ricans began identifying themselves as New Yoricans or Ricans — people who claim pride in being Puerto Rican but who acknowledge their New York soul. Implied in these terms is an acceptance of a non-white and ghetto status, with all its positive and negative consequences (this step would have been an impossible one for many Puerto Ricans reared on the island). For Puerto Ricans, this is the start of a new, self-defined position — an attempt to remain a unified whole and evolve from our own roots, between blacks and whites.

It is not clear where this change will lead, or what political implications it will have for Puerto Ricans. However, the commonly predicted routes for Puerto Rican identity-resolution have changed. For it is no longer clear that "black" Puerto Ricans will assimilate into black American culture and that "white" Puerto Ricans will disappear in the white suburbs, while the various beiges, tans and browns in between will hold on as the standard bearers of the New York Puerto Rican culture. Although these channels of assimilation still exist and exert pressures upon Puerto Ricans choosing and creating mind worlds and life spaces, it is no longer probable that people will follow these paths without question.

NOTES

1. And assuming in both instances that culture is held constant, i.e., an American white or black may not be judged within the Puerto Rican cultural framework. However, in Puerto Rico, the white-appearing offspring of an interracial American couple may still be seen as Negro because that is the culture he bears; that is how he has been socialized.

2. Most authors take the position that racial classification in Puerto Rico is class-influenced. But Harris (1970) concludes that color categories in Brazil (which are similar to those in Puerto Rico) cannot be seen in American terms.

3. There would probably be disagreement between Puerto Ricans and Americans on whether some "*blancos*" were the equivalent of whites in the U.S.

4. Felipe Luciano, former member of the Young Lords, describes Puerto Ricans as the "Rainbow People."

5. This term implies that claiming that no prejudice exists may in itself be a prejudicial act.

6. These same issues were underscored in the recent contesting of the U.S. Census count of Puerto Ricans. Puerto Rican groups demanded that third–

generation Puerto Ricans should be included in the count, pointing out that blacks are counted as blacks regardless of generation. The census considered Puerto Ricans as it has previous immigrant groups. However, as one community leader stated: "We are still considered Puerto Ricans no matter how long we are here." New York Times, July 3, 1972.

7. Those in this category going to a lighter categorization tended to be more favorably inclined to assimilation.

8. Though we know Puerto Ricans with obvious African ancestry are categorized as blacks, we don't really have data on how other Puerto Ricans are viewed when it is known they are Puerto Rican. Personal experiences of Puerto Ricans in New York indicate, however, that New Yorkers perceive Puerto Ricans as darker once they know the person is Puerto Rican.

9. I believe this was true not just for Puerto Ricans but for other "unmeltable ethnics" as well.

REFERENCE

Harris, Marvin. "Referential ambiguity in the calculus of Brazilian racial identity," in Norman E. Whitten, Jr. and John F. Szwed, eds., Afro-American Anthropology, New York: The Free Press. 1970.

Economic Survival
in New York City

Introduction

This article is one of the first to examine the political and economic structural factors that were impacting upon the Puerto Rican community during the sixties and seventies. While earlier works tended to focus on the deficiencies of the (im)migrants or their inability to adjust, this article pointed to forces beyond their control that affected economic survival, such as the suburbanization of jobs, automation, robotization, the decline of the manufacturing sector (where Puerto Ricans were concentrated), and the growth of the service sector. This type of analysis was subsequently employed in understanding other groups, for instance blue-collar white workers in deindustrializing areas of the economy. Subsequent analyses of the migration of Puerto Ricans and other groups had to contend with the actuality of these factors.

The article also focused on dimensions not generally discussed in analyses of the Puerto Rican community but that impacted on economic survival, such as barriers to union membership, racial and ethnic prejudice, inadequate educational opportunities, and the role of government. Finally, it addressed the issue of dividends the New York City economy garnered as a result of the Puerto Rican migration. In other words, the argument that is heard today with regard to the contributions that immigrants make to the nation's economy was initially put forth in this article. At a time when generally only the welfare costs of Puerto Ricans were discussed, the article made it clear that New York City's claim to be the "garment capital of the world" had rested on Puerto Rican shoulders. It also clarified what most members of the community already knew—and what had been earlier articulated in community reports. This was that the great majority of Puerto Ricans were *not* on welfare. In so doing, it challenged what was then a prevailing assumption.

ECONOMIC SURVIVAL IN NEW YORK CITY
by Clara E. Rodríguez

This paper reviews a number of factors that contributed to the socioeconomic positioning of the Puerto Rican community in New York City between 1950 and 1970. These factors are: automation, suburbanization, sectoral decline, blue-collar structural unemployment, racial and ethnic prejudice, restrictive union policies, inadequate educational opportunities and the virtual exclusion of Puerto Ricans from government employment. The paper also looks at what the New York economy gained from the Puerto Rican migration, i.e., the "positive-tipping-point" role that Puerto Ricans played in business and industry. Lastly, the paper analyzes welfare as the economy's response to the situation described.

Although this analysis is far from comprehensive, it is an attempt to answer the question of why Puerto Ricans are on the bottom rung. It differs from similar analyses in that it examines factors outside of the Puerto Rican psyche (e.g., predilection for work or cultural attitudes toward political dependency) and because it attempts to go beyond the simplistic explanations generally offered of low-skill levels and low educational attainment to an examination of external structural factors impacting upon the community. In short, the paper focuses on what we're up against, instead of what's wrong with us.

Socioeconomic Positioning

Many of the myriad aspects of the Puerto Rican community in

Dr. Clara E. Rodríguez is Professor of Sociology, Fordham College at Lincoln Center, New York, N.Y. An earlier version of this paper was published in History Task Force, Centro de Estudios Puertorriqueños, Labor MIgration Under Capitalism, copyright 1979 by the Research Foundation of the City University of New York. Reprinted by permission of monthly Review Press.

New York have been examined, discussed, deplored, or excused without sufficient attention being paid to how the New York economy has impacted on Puerto Ricans. Generally, the economy has been superficially analyzed and then only as a push or pull factor in the migration of Puerto Ricans to New York.[1] The role of the economy in determining what happened after Puerto Ricans migrated to New York has yet to be fully examined in the growing body of literature on Puerto Ricans.

It is clear from available data that Puerto Ricans have not been evenly integrated into the New York economy.[2] Comparing the occupational distribution of male Puerto Ricans between 1950 and 1970 (Table 1), we see that relative to blacks and the total population, Puerto Rican males have been, and are, disproportionately represented in the blue-collar occupations. This disproportionate concentration vis-a-vis other groups held constant between 1950 and 1970 — despite a significant decrease (from 61.0 percent to 51.3 percent) in the proportion of Puerto Ricans in the blue-collar jobs between 1960 and 1970 (Rodríguez, 1973). That is, although the proportion of Puerto Rican blue-collar workers decreased, it still remains substantially higher than the comparable black and total population groups.

This decrease in blue-collar workers between 1960 and 1970 seems to be accounted for by an increase in service-sector workers rather than by significant gains in white-collar employment. Thus, with respect to white-collar jobs, Puerto Rican males have the smallest proportion of white-collar workers of all three groups: 27.2 percent compared to 32.5 percent for blacks and 51 percent for the total population. When we look at the figures in more detail, we see that there has been greater mobility of Puerto Rican females into white-collar occupations than of Puerto Rican males.[3] The mere analysis of the proportions of blue-collar and white-collar workers in the labor force is not itself sufficient to indicate the relative success of Puerto Rican economic integration, for some blue-collar workers earn more than many white-collar workers. Thus, it is necessary to consider income differentials by occupation.

Looking at Table 2, we see that within each occupational group, Puerto Rican males and females are paid less than black or white males or females. No data are available by specific occupations — for example, doctors, or plumbers — but the figures indicate fairly clearly

Table 1. Occupational Distribution of Employed Males, by Racial/Ethnic Group, New York SMSA, 1950-1970

Occupation	Puerto Rican			Black			Total Population		
	1950	1960	1970	1950	1960	1970	1950	1960[a]	1970
Total Employed	50,445	136,000	153,000	187,215	233,584	358,641	2,658,143	2,842,000	2,809,000
Percent	100.0	100.0	100.0	98.2	100.0	100.1	98.8	100.0	100.0
White Collar	18.0	18.1	27.2	21.4	27.0	32.5	45.9	47.9	51.0
Blue Collar	53.4	61.0	51.3	50.4	50.8	47.8	41.8	41.4	36.8
Service Workers	28.5	20.6	21.2	26.0	22.0	19.5	10.7	10.5	12.0
Farm Workers	0.1	0.3	0.3	0.4	0.3	0.3	0.4	0.3	0.2

[a]These data do not include the "occupation-not-reported" category.

Source: 1950 U.S. Census of Population, Volume II, Characteristics of the Population, Part 32, Table 77; Special Report P-E 30, Puerto Ricans in the Continental U.S., Table 5; 1960 U.S. Census of Population, Special Reports, PC(2)-ID, Table 11; 1960 U.S. Census of Population, Part 34, Table 74; 1970 U.S. Census of Population, General Social and Economic Characteristics, PC(1)-C34, Tables 86 and 99.

that Puerto Ricans have only marginally been integrated into the New York economy.

Table 2. Median Earnings in 1969 by Major Occupational Groups of Males and Females with Earnings, Sixteen Years and Over, by Racial/Ethnic Group, New York City

	Total	White	Black	Puerto Rican
Male				
Professional, managerial, and kindred workers	$10,995	$11,400	$8,046	$7,040
Craftsmen, foremen, and kindred workers	8,174	8,520	6,770	6,238
Operatives, including transport	6,556	6,767	6,187	5,148
Laborers, except farm	6,577	6,986	5,816	5,051
Total male experienced labor force	7,679	8,140	6,241	5,430
Female				
Clerical and kindred workers	5,360	5,464	4,867	4,563
Operatives, including transport	3,741	3,715	3,854	3,651
Total female experienced labor force	4,978	5,131	4,572	3,861

Source: U.S. Department of Labor, Manpower Administration, "Summary Manpower Indicators for New York City."

If we look at unemployment rates for Puerto Rican males between 1950 and 1970, we see the same lack of integration. In each year the unemployment rate for Puerto Rican males in New York was about double that of whites and higher than that of blacks. For the years 1950, 1960 and 1970, respectively, unemployment among Puerto Rican males was 10.6, 9.9 and 6.2 percent, while among "nonwhites," it was 8.4, 6.9 and 5.4 percent, and among "others," it was 5.1, 4.3, and 3.9 percent. Had the labor force participation rates of Puerto Rican males in the New York Standard Metropolitan Statistical Area (SMSA) not declined substantially between 1960 and 1970, the unemployment rate would have been even higher.

Since the labor market is the prime determinant of income in the United States it is not surprising to find that Puerto Ricans are poorer than either whites or blacks. The proportion of families with incomes below $7,000 (the low-income budget line) is 64 percent for Puerto Ricans, as compared with 29 percent for whites and 49 percent for blacks, while the proportion of families in poverty (under $3,700) was similarly skewed, with 30 percent of Puerto Rican families being thus classified in 1970, compared with 12 percent of all races and 21 percent of blacks. The median family income of Puerto Ricans has also lagged a considerable distance behind that of other groups since 1950: in New York City in 1970 it was $5,575, compared to $10,424 for whites and $7,150 for blacks.

Factors Affecting Puerto Ricans

What are the root causes of Puerto Rican high unemployment, skewed occupational distribution, and low income? If we examine the economy and its relation to Puerto Ricans, we find a number of factors that contribute substantially to these phenomena. These include automation, suburbanization, sectoral decline, blue-collar structural unemployment, racial and ethnic prejudice, restrictive union policies, inadequate educational opportunities, and the near exclusion of Puerto Ricans from government employment.

In a nutshell, here is how these factors operate and interact. Automation and the movement of surviving blue-collar jobs to the suburbs, the South, and to other countries have caused a sectoral decline in the number of manufacturing jobs available in New York City. Since these trends occurred more rapidly than out-migration or the retraining of blue-collar workers to fill white-collar jobs, a severe problem of blue-collar structural unemployment arose. Because of racial and ethnic prejudice, restrictive union policies, inadequate educational opportunities, and the virtual exclusion of Puerto Ricans from government employment, Puerto Ricans bore the brunt of this blue-collar structural unemployment. Let us now examine, in more depth, these trends and their impact upon Puerto Ricans in New York.

Automation. Automation is one of the more significant changes the economy was undergoing during the height of the Puerto Rican migration. The effects of automation upon the black labor force have already been examined fairly closely (Wilhelm, 1971). Given the similarities of the black and Puerto Rican labor forces, the same line of analysis is applicable to Puerto Ricans. Thus, it is argued that the effects of automation are and were very dramatically felt in the blue-collar workforce, and since a large proportion of black (and an even larger proportion of Puerto Rican) workers are blue-collar, the black labor force has been more affected by automation than the white labor force.

Since Puerto Ricans have the highest proportion of blue-collar laborers in New York City, they have been the most affected.

Suburbanization. Paralleling automation was a trend toward increased suburbanization of industry, which placed many blue-collar jobs in the suburbs. If Puerto Ricans came to know about suburban job openings, transportation to the jobs, when available, was expensive in terms of money and time—adding one or two hours to each workday.[4] In addition, the industries in the suburbs already had a substantial pool of labor among the suburbanites who had moved nearby or would soon flee the city to get those jobs. Thus the jobs in the suburbs were fairly unattainable to Puerto Ricans, while the attainable jobs in the city were few. Moreover, the numbers of city jobs held by suburbanites who commute into the city is very high. Although many of the jobs held by commuters are white-collar, and thus may not be immediately open to many Puerto Ricans, they do further delimit the opportunity structure for Puerto Ricans.

The effect that suburbanization of industry and people had on Puerto Ricans was not just limited to employment. It depleted the tax base of the cities. With a shrinking middle class, the revenues collected proved insufficient to cover the services usually provided. At the same time, the city, with its younger, poorer population had greater demands put on its services. Thus, while the Puerto Ricans had greater needs, the city had less money.

Sectoral Decline. Automation and suburbanization combined to cause sectoral decline. Sectoral decline is not a recent phenomenon in New York. Vernon and Hoover (1962) found that between 1929 and 1939, and between 1947 and 1956, New York City lost ground with respect to its growing industries, while it held on to its declining ones. However, the problem has become more acute in recent years, thereby adversely and significantly affecting Puerto Ricans. A dramatic example can be seen in manufacturing. In 1960, manufacturing employed 60 percent of the Puerto Rican workforce. In the decade that followed, manufacturing jobs in the city decreased by 173,000 (Bureau of Labor Statistics, 1972). This loss was not offset by an increase in low-level service jobs, the other major area of Puerto Rican workforce concentration. Thus, as would be expected and as the U.S. Commission on Civil Rights (1972) found, sectoral decline became an important contributory cause of high unemployment among Puerto Ricans.

Even in 1970, the majority of Puerto Ricans were to be found in declining sectors while the growth sectors employed few Puerto Ricans. Despite the decline in jobs in manufacturing, this area has continued to hold significant proportions of the Puerto Rican labor force. Even in 1968-1969, as the U.S. Commission on Civil Rights noted, Puerto Ricans in poor neighborhoods were still found in overwhelming numbers in manufacturing. In 1970, 60 percent of the manufacturing jobs paid less than was required to sustain a decent, minimum standard of living as determined by the Bureau of Labor Statistics (New York Times, November 5, 1972: 43).

Blue-Collar Structural Unemployment. Sectoral decline combined with insufficient educational opportunities and retraining of blue-collar workers to produce blue-collar structural unemployment, which has been an almost chronic condition of the economy for about a decade. In simplest terms, the problem is an excess of blue-collar workers relative to blue-collar jobs and a scarcity of white-collar workers for an excess of white-collar jobs. The Regional Plan Association finds this to be one of the main problems of the regional economy. Puerto Ricans, again because of the labor-force composition, have been and are bearing the brunt of this structural problem.

The trends in this area indicate a further deterioration of the situation. When the labor-force composition of Puerto Ricans (and blacks) is compared against the present and projected demand for blue-collar, white-collar and service jobs, it is clear that blacks and Puerto Ricans do and will suffer the most from the problem of blue-collar structural unemployment (Regional Plan Association, 1972). The unemployment could be diminished if more Puerto Ricans (and blacks) entered the white-collar than the blue-collar labor force. "However," as the Regional Plan Association (1972: 3) states, "it appears that public schools in the regions' older cities and manpower training programmes both tend to channel blacks and Puerto Ricans into blue-collar work." Thus it appears that New York's educational institutions and even its manpower agencies contribute to the problem.

Trade Unions. The environment* in which these trends have been occurring has been strongly affected by the unions. Formerly a vehicle of minority mobility, they now function to keep out minorities. Having battled the older entrenched ethnic groups for an occupational niche, the newer ethnic groups now use the unions as a means of securing their positions. Although data on unions are very difficult to come by, it is fairly clear that with the exception of low-level jobs in garment factories and food services, most skilled or craft unions are closed to Puerto Ricans.[5] Thus, many Puerto Ricans' benefits and pay raises may be inferior to those of other workers doing the same job. The result of union blockages has been the growth of freelance, nonunionized, and therefore lower-paid, Puerto Rican plumbers, painters, plasterers, electricians, etc.

Racial and Ethnic Prejudice. Also influencing the effects of these trends on Puerto Ricans were racial barriers. Although ethnic differences often presented a barrier to previous immigrant groups, Puerto Ricans have had to contend with institutionalized racism, as well as institutionalized hostility to ethnic differences. For although, officially, only nine percent of Puerto Ricans are categorized as black (according to census self-classification), a much larger proportion appears racially nonwhite to Americans and will thus experience racial discrimination (State Charter Revision Commission for New York City, 1973). Thus, racism is an important factor affecting the labor market for Puerto Ricans and accounts significantly for the severe distortions in resource allocation to which Puerto Ricans have been subject.

The more "objective" economic factors which have adversely influenced the economic integration of Puerto Ricans into New York City were automation, suburbanization, sectoral decline, and restrictive union policies, factors which were not present to any significant degree during the migrations of previous immigrant groups. Yet these factors have typified the regional New York economy (and to some extent the U.S. economy) in the last decades. When Puerto Ricans and southern blacks were arriving in great numbers, these factors interacted with each other and with racial and ethnic prejudice to create an economic environment inimical to Puerto Rican economic integration.

Inadequate Educational Opportunities. Although it must be admitted that there are educational differentials between Puerto Ricans, blacks and whites in New York City, these are not sufficient by themselves to explain the occupational patterning, the income differentials by occupation, and the extremely high unemployment rates to which Puerto Ricans are subject. This is to say nothing of the causes of these educational differentials, such as the inferior schooling Puerto Ricans receive in New York City schools, and received as a result of U.S. educational policies in Puerto Rico.[6]

Furthermore, if we compare the educational attainments of the New York City population in 1970, we see that although there are differences between ethnic groups, they are not as great as the above figures on income and occupation would lead us to expect. For example, close to 53 percent of the white population in New York City 25 years and over are not high school graduates, compared to 80 percent of Puerto Ricans within this age group. Does this justify a median income about two times as large (New York City Manpower Area Planning Council, 1974)?

Government Employment as a Last Resort. Wilhelm (1971) notes that the government has assumed an increasingly larger role as an employer of blacks. Because of this, black unemployment has been kept from increasing too dramatically. Government, however, has not intervened in the same way with respect to the Puerto Rican community, for in 1970 only 12 percent of Puerto Ricans were employed by government, compared to 23 percent of blacks, while local government employed only 7 percent of Puerto Ricans as compared with 15 percent of blacks (U.S. Bureau of the Census, 1973: Tables 80,92,98). Thus, government has not served as an employer of last resort to Puerto Ricans.

A recent extensive survey of municipal government was so appalled at the high under-representation of Puerto Ricans in New York City government that it specifically recommended that, "Utmost priority should be given by the Department of Personnel and all agencies to recruiting members of the Puerto Rican community" (NYC Commission on Human Rights, 1973). No other ethnic group was so "honored."

Summary. In summary, though Mayor Wagner went to San

Juan to tell Puerto Ricans that the mainland needed migrants to fill jobs (N.Y. Times, June 27, 1964), Puerto Ricans were to meet the sad realities of job placement in New York. This job market had a decreasing demand, for low-skilled jobs were being eliminated by automation, others were protected by unions, others were moving to the suburbs, while suburbanites were taking many jobs in the city. Thus, Puerto Ricans moved into the only jobs available: low-wage work in the service sector (as waiters, kitchen help, porters, and hospital workers), and in light manufacturing (as sewing-machine operators). In short, they were the jobs nobody else wanted. These tended to be low-paying and the sectors in which they were found tended to be declining or unstable.

Not only were jobs few, low-paying, and often insecure, but once a job was obtained, mobility was also poor. Where could you go from being a sewing-machine operator? Perhaps to the post of supervisor, earning $10 more a week. Similarly, in the food trades, the ladder to success started with dishwasher and usually ended with waiter. The few chef positions available were usually reserved for people who had more in the way of "public relations"—as, for example, French chefs did. Most jobs were deadend jobs.

Migration Dividends to the Economy

Despite the depressed position of Puerto Ricans in the New York economy, Puerto Ricans were and are crucial to its proper functioning. Even though the jobs do not pay much, they are important. Someone has to serve the tables and wash the dishes of the white-collar workers. It is in this context that we must see the exploited, yet crucial, position of Puerto Ricans. The textile industry provides one example of the crucial role Puerto Ricans played in an industry vital to New York's economy.

New York accounts for 70 percent of all dollar sales of clothing in the United States at the wholesale level (New York Times, 11/26/72). Garment manufacturers produce and sell more than $7 billion in apparel each year. Although the total number of garment firms has declined over the years, the total dollar volume of business has risen. As with industrialization in farming, the remaining firms are larger and financially stronger.

Some scholars contend that but for the Puerto Rican migration,

New York City would not have been able to hold on to this very important industry.[7] Puerto Ricans have, in a sense, provided a "positive tipping point." Without this source of cheap labor many more firms would have left the city; those that stayed would have had to reduce their production. In this sense, New York's claim to be the garment capital of the world has rested upon Puerto Rican shoulders.

The Harvard study of the New York metropolitan region took note of this role in the 1950's:

> The rate of Puerto Rican migration to New York is one of the factors that determine how long and how successfully the New York metropolitan region will retain industries which are under competitive pressure from other areas. To the extent that some of these industries have hung on in the area, they have depended on recently arrived Puerto Rican workers, who have entered the job market of the New York area at the rate of about 13,000 each year (Vernon, 1960).

Puerto Rican migration was not at a consistently high level in the 1960's, and this may affect the numbers entering the job market. However, the rate of second-generation entry into the job market and the rate of non-Puerto Rican migration to the suburbs may compensate for decreased Puerto Rican migration. Thus, Puerto Ricans may retain their role as "tippers" who enable or encourage firms to stay or to grow. Low wages for Puerto Ricans continue and thus provide a main incentive in this respect.

Although figures are not available for the hotel and restaurant industry, it would seem that a similar phenomenon occurred there. If anything, the role of "tippers" would be accentuated because Puerto Ricans made up a greater percentage of employees in this field.[8] To some extent, the growing numbers of blacks and Puerto Ricans in health and hospital services might be seen as a forthcoming, and parallel, phenomenon. In this case, however, government intervenes sufficiently to ensure that blacks and Puerto Ricans are recruited into these occupations. These services can be considered to be almost public utilities that do not have the option of leaving the city, but of growing or deteriorating.

Although at present unresearched, Puerto Rican migration has also undoubtedly had a large role in moving previous immigrant groups up the economic ladder. Twenty-five years ago garment workers were predominantly Jewish and Italian; now Puerto Ricans and other new immigrants have taken their place. Although mortality accounts for a large part of the decline of Jewish and Italian employees, their children are seldom found as workers in the garment trades. Nor are they usually to be found in similar low-paying occupations. The question, of course, is whether a larger proportion of them would have had to take these low-paying jobs despite probable increased education and language skills. This question remains unanswered. But the fact remains that Puerto Ricans took these jobs and that the sons of previous immigrant groups in the garment trades took better jobs and perhaps became owners and managers in expanded firms. Whatever the cause, the ethnic queuing occurred.[9]

The significance of the manufacturing industries to the welfare of the city cannot be overemphasized. There is a renewed awareness of the importance of the garment industry as the largest employer in the city. (The garment industry employs more people than any other type of manufacturing, providing a total annual payroll of $1.5 billion.)[10]

Puerto Ricans, and now an increasingly large number of undocumented workers, provide the unacknowledged, but indispensable role of perhaps all previous immigrant groups — that of supporting the base of the economic system.[11]

Welfare: The Economy's Response

Given the low incomes, high unemployment, and insecure jobs held by Puerto Ricans, we would expect to see an extremely high rate of welfare recipients among the Puerto Rican population in New York. In fact, it is not as high as might be expected given the parameters of Puerto Rican poverty. In 1970, 30 percent of Puerto Rican families in New York were on welfare; that is, fully 70 percent were completely self-supporting. Of those families eligible for welfare, that is, with incomes below the poverty level, only 56 percent were on welfare.[12] But the whole issue must be seen within a wider context in order to grasp the full significance of the role the economy has played in placing Puerto Ricans on welfare.

Welfare can be seen to be a contracting economy's response to structural and sectoral unemployment.[13] In addition to taking up the slack in the economy, it also provides jobs for clerical and higher skilled workers—the welfare establishment—while it cools out what may otherwise be an unbearable and explosive situation for the unemployed. At the same time, it tends to subsidize the low-wage industrial sector and the landlord class, which is a direct beneficiary of welfare rent payments (Valentine, 1972). Given the fears associated with color in this country, it is not surprising that welfare has come to be used as an economic policy. That is to say, to some extent individuals are encouraged by the system to apply for welfare; this is done as a means of handling the more difficult structural economic problems.

The system encourages this through the economic factors already noted, for example, unemployment, low incomes, low-status jobs. But it also encourages it directly through the liberalization of welfare policy. Note, for example, those measures that were instituted between 1960 and 1970 when the welfare rolls swelled: doing away with "need" or proof of eligibility, investigator visits, and the man-in-the-home clause; rising rates of support; and support for drug addicts. The fact that welfare funds are mainly federal (50 percent) and state (25 percent) gives added incentive for the city government to cope with its economic problems in this way (State Charter Revision Commission, 1973).

In this period of economic contraction, Puerto Ricans, as the poorest of the poor, have been shunted into welfare — but not more than in proportion to income. Their resistance has been substantial, however, for 70 percent have managed to sustain their families without welfare on extremely low wages, and much higher percentages managed to do so prior to 1960.[14] But for increasing proportions, the only way to survive is welfare. It is in the dilution of alternatives that the system forces Puerto Ricans into welfare.

NOTES

1. On this point, see Friedlander (1965); Fleisher (1961); Pantoja (1972); Glazer and Moynihan (1970); Senior and Watkins (1966).
2. The following figures are, in the main, census figures. There is a great deal of truth in the charges made against the Census Bureau with regard to undercounting, miscounting, and resulting inaccuracies. The actual number of Puerto Ricans in New York City may be closer to 1.2 million, a full 50 percent more than the 800,000 estimated by the census. Despite the very valid objections to the census figures, they are unfortunately the only ones available for the present analysis. They are used mainly to indicate relationships, not exact representations, thus avoiding to some

degree the objections raised. However, they probably understate what will be seen to be fairly significant contrasts between blacks, Puerto Ricans, and whites.

3. The effect this is having on the traditionally strong patriarchal Puerto Rican family structure is an important issue that has not been given sufficient attention in the literature.

4. The American Transit Authority estimated the nationwide average cost for an inner-city resident to travel to the suburbs for his or her job to be $15 per month in 1968. In New York, the estimate for transportation from Harlem to Farmingdale, L.I. was $40 per month in the same year. See Will and Vatter (1970). This does not take into account waiting time, and schedules are usually geared to facilitate the mass of suburbanites coming into the city for work and not vice versa.

5. Tabb (1972) presents data (limited to referral unions) that bear out the contention that Puerto Ricans are vastly under-represented in certain unions, especially the craft unions.

6. Indeed, as a recent report makes clear, at every level of education, the percentage of families with an income below the poverty level in 1968 was higher for Puerto Ricans than for the black or total populations. See U.S. Department of Labor, Bureau of Labor Statistics (1975: 118). The following references discuss the relationship between educational policy and practice and Puerto Ricans: Rodríguez (1974); and Rodríguez Bou (1966).

7. See, for example, Senior and Watkins (1966: 689-765), Helfgott, et al. (1959) and Vernon (1960).

8. For exact numbers of Spanish-surnamed by industry and by occupation within industry, see Equal Employment Opportunity Commission (1966).

9. The owners of garment industries remain predominantly Jewish, with a sprinkling of Italians. See New York Times, November 26, 1972, Section 3, p. 2.

10. Ibid., p. 1.

11. A recent article in the New York Times (March 19, 1979, p. 1) estimated that there were between 350,000 and 1.5 million undocumented workers in New York City, with the majority of these employed in the manufacturing and service sectors. The extent to which this influx of new lower-skilled workers has impacted upon the Puerto Rican labor force is as yet unresearched.

12. According to former social-services employees, many non-Puerto Rican Spanish-speaking people pass as Puerto Ricans in order to get on welfare. This to some extent inflates the figures.

13. This concept of welfare has a number of antecedents. See Marx's analysis

51

of public concessions to workers and the poor (1970, vol. 1: 278-97). For historical evidence supporting the relationship between welfare and fluctuations in the economy, see Piven and Cloward (1971) and Gordon (1969).

14. U.S. Bureau of the Census (1973, Tables 90, 95, and 101). These figures are for the whole year, and so the figures at any one time during the year will be less.

REFERENCES

Equal Employment Opportunity Commission. Job Patterns for Minorities and Women in Private Industry. 1966.

Fleisher, Belton H. "Some Economic Aspects of Puerto Rican Migration to the United States." Unpublished doctoral dissertation, Stanford University. 1961.

Friedlander, Stanley. Labor, Migration and Economic Growth. Cambridge, Mass.: MIT Press. 1965.

Glazer, Nathan and Daniel Moynihan. Beyond the Melting Pot. Cambridge, Mass.: MIT Press. 1970.

Gordon, David M. "Income and welfare in New York City." The Public Interest 16. 1969.

Helfgott, Roy B., et al. Made In New York. Cambridge, Mass.: Harvard University Press. 1959.

Marx, Karl. "The Struggle for the Normal Working-Day. Compulsory Limitation by Law of the Working-Time," in Capital, vol. I. New York: International Publishers. 1970.

New York City Commission on Human Rights. The Employment of Minorities, Women, and the Handicapped in City Government. 1973.

New York City Manpower Area Planning Council. Comprehensive Manpower Plan for New York City, Fiscal Year 1974. New York: Office of the Mayor. 1974.

Pantoja, Antonia. "Puerto Rican Migration," in Preliminary Report to the U.S. Commission on the Civil Rights of Puerto Ricans. 1972.

Piven, Frances Fox and Richard Cloward. Regulating the Poor. New York: Vintage Books. 1971.

Regional Plan Association. "Linking Skills, Jobs, and Housing in the New York Urban Region." New York. 1972.

Rodríguez, Clara. The Ethnic Queue in the United States: The Case of Puerto Ricans. San Francisco: R & E Research Associates. 1973.

———. "Puerto Ricans and the New York City school system." Urban Review (June). 1974.

Rodríguez Bou, Ismael. "Significant Factors in the Development of Education in Puerto Rico," in U.S.-Puerto Rico Commission on the Status of Puerto Rico, Status of Puerto Rico: Selected Background Studies. Washington, D.C.: U.S. Government Printing Office. 1966.

Senior, Clarence and Donald Watkins. "Toward a Balance Sheet of Puerto Rican Migration," in U.S.-Puerto Rico Commission on the Status of Puerto Rico, Status of Puerto Rico: Selected Background Studies. Washington, D.C.: U.S. Government Printing Office. 1966.

State Charter Revision Commission for New York City. "New York City Today: Demographic and Economic Background Information." Staff report, December. 1973.

Tabb, William K. "Puerto Ricans in New York City: A Study of Economic and Social Conditions." Bureau of Labor Statistics, New York Regional Office, unpublished report. 1972.

U.S. Bureau of the Census. Census of Population: 1970, General Social and Economic Characteristics. PC (1)-C34. Washington, D.C.: U.S. Government Printing Office. 1973.

U.S. Commission on Civil Rights. "Demographic, Social, and Economic Characteristics of New York City and the New York Metropolitan Area." Hearings on the Civil Rights of Puerto Ricans. Staff report, February. 1972.

U.S. Department of Labor, Bureau of Labor Statistics. The New York Puerto Rican: Patterns of Work Experience. Regional Report No. 19, Poverty Area Profiles. 1972.

A Socioeconomic Profile of Puerto Rican New Yorkers, Regional Report No. 46, July. 1975.

Valentine, Charles. "Black Studies and Anthropology: Scholarly and Political Interests in Afro-American Culture." Addison Wesley Modular Publications, Module 15. 1972.

Vernon, Raymond. Metropolis, 1985. Cambridge, Mass.: Harvard University Press. 1960.

Vernon, Raymond and Edgar M. Hoover. Anatomy of a Metropolis. New York: Doubleday-Anchor. 1962.

Wilhelm, Sidney M. Who Needs the Negro? New York: Doubleday-Anchor. 1971.

Will, Robert and Harold Vatter, eds. Poverty in Affluence. New York: Harcourt, Brace and World. 1970.

Survival of Puerto Rican Women in New York Before World War II

Introduction

This seminal essay delineates the role of women in creating and expanding the community at a critical juncture in the historical evolution of the Puerto Rican diaspora. As underpaid workers in the informal economy, childcare providers and administrators of in-house room and board enterprises, they bolstered familial survival and extended kinship bonds. In subsequent work, Sánchez Korrol continues to document the history of Puerto Rican women in a number of different arenas: as community organizers; in religious vocations; at the forefront of the bilingual education movement; and in positions of leadership.

As women's roles in the home and community undergo redefinition, so too are they beginning to garner well-deserved recognition in the literature for their prior leadership and participation in founding influential community institutions and organizations. Included among these are the Puerto Rican Forum, the Puerto Rican Family Institute, ASPIRA, the Puerto Rican Educators Association, as well as the establishment of bilingual education programs in the public schools and university-based departments and programs in Puerto Rican Studies.

Without doubt, the research on Puerto Rican women as key factors in creating, defining and maintaining community, whether within the context of family, workforce participation, as teachers and other professionals, in popular education programs, as community activists, or as politicians continues at an even pace. The ten-year period from 1981 to 1992 witnessed the writing of some thirty dissertations that focused on Puerto Rican women. The work of scholars Edna Acosta Belén

(1979), Altagracia Ortiz (ND), Rina Benmayor (1987; 1992), and a host of other researchers have bestowed agency and illuminating insights that serve to empower women and lay to rest stereotypical notions about the roles enacted by *Puertorriqueñas*. Their studies highlight issues of class, race, language and identity, an affirmation of cultural citizenship and the migration experience.

More recently, scholars based in Puerto Rico and others from U.S. communities have begun to create regional and intellectual spaces where collaborative efforts and comparative perspectives may be fostered in the research. Their work attempts to erase the boundaries between the island and mainland experience, bridging the geographic halves that comprise the experiential totality of Puerto Rican women's reality. Through professional associations like the Puerto Rican Studies Association, women scholars have succeeded in organizing working groups that will ultimately expand the research agenda to include comparative studies on Puerto Rican and other Latinas.

SURVIVAL OF PUERTO RICAN WOMEN IN NEW YORK BEFORE WORLD WAR II

by Virginia Sánchez Korrol

The first Puerto Rican settlements of consequence in New York City did not materialize until the 1920's. Along with other Hispanic immigrants, Puerto Ricans lived in Manhattan's Chelsea section from 15th to 25th Street, with another concentration around 116th Street in Harlem. Other communities flourished around the Navy Yard and Borough Hall sections of Brooklyn. Women held a special place in these early settlements, often providing links between the island and the New York enclaves. Pivotal factors in retaining ethnicity through the transmission of language and culture within familial settings, women also functioned as part of an information network. Referred to as "the family intelligence service," this network acclimated incoming migrants to the intricacies of the receiving society (Senior and Watkins, 1966; Smith, 1976). Over the factory sewing machines or on apartment-house stoops, in the *bodegas* or in the privacy of their own homes, women exchanged information on housing, jobs, folk remedies, the best places to shop, their churches and their children's schools. What has usually been characterized as idle female chatter essentially provided the tools for handling the unfamiliar situation.

Although some Puerto Rican women in the early New York settlements participated in community groups and volunteer organizations, many preferred being young mothers who cherished the Hispanic family traditions which dictated women's place within the home. But others, faced with the economic realities of the predominantly poor *colonias*, found ways to combine child-raising with

Dr. Virginia Sánchez Korrol is Professor and Chair of the Department of Puerto Rican Studies, Brooklyn College, City University of New York. An earlier version of this paper was published by Caribbean Review. Research support provided by a grant from the Ford Foundation is greatfully acknowledged.

gainful employment.

An analysis of the 1925 New York State Census revealed that out of 7,322 Hispanic individuals living in Manhattan's 16th, 17th, 18th and 19th Assembly Districts in Harlem, 48 percent were female. These districts were generally accepted as representing heavy Hispanic concentrations and provide a substantive profile of the Hispanic community (New York State Manuscript Census, 1925). Based on census information, 75 oral interviews with working-class women who lived in New York City during the pre-World-War-II years, and other sources, Puerto Rican females in New York emerged not as stereotypical Latins relegated to second-class status bound by children, church and home, but as active, vibrant women determined to keep family life intact while shouldering their share of financial burdens. This paper focuses on the integration of Puerto Rican women into the economic networks of New York City and the enterprises which they adopted to avoid conflicts with their traditional view of family life.

Housewives and children comprised the bulk of the female population in the four Assembly Districts previously cited: 42 percent of the females living in that area listed their occupation as "housewife" in the census, 29 percent were female children and students and the remaining 29 percent worked outside the home. The group listed as "housewives and children" had spent a comparatively short period in the New York settlements: 45 percent had been in the United States less than three years. Furthermore, 79 percent of the female population in the four districts were under 35 years of age. All of this presents a picture of the woman migrant of the mid-1920's as someone fairly young who did not work outside the home and who had not been in New York for any length of time (New York State Manuscript Census, 1925).[1]

The role of Puerto Rican women in New York communities during the 1920's and 1930's was an extension of the role they played in their island society. During the early periods women were expected to stay at home caring for husband and children, but the term "housewife" was open to interpretation when applied to Puerto Rican women. While they basically thought of themselves as women of the home (*mujeres de la casa*), many engaged in activities designed to supplement family incomes, and various home-centered economic ventures emerged in response to their economic needs.

Piecework

One of the major forms of home enterprise for women was piecework, which included making lampshades, hats, artificial flowers and jewelry, as well as embroidering, crocheting and sewing. Piecework was essentially the same as had been practiced in Puerto Rico and enjoyed popularity among early migrants, who were familiar with its advantages. In Puerto Rico, where by the 1920's women constituted close to 25 percent of the work force, they had become essential to this type of industry as early as 1910.[2] Nurtured in a tradition of quality needlecrafts for generations, Puerto Rican women almost always possessed skills in sewing and crocheting. In fact, these skills were taught in Puerto Rican schools in the primary grades. One interviewee recalls attending a sewing school operated by two women in the neighborhood where she learned embroidery and lace working before her tenth birthday. Another told of her experiences in the factories of Mayagüez, where she learned the trade and skills she brought to the factories of New York.

Piecework ranked among the earliest job experiences of many Puerto Rican women in New York City. Some engaged in this form of employment because there were young children at home who needed their mother's care; others combined it with factory work, especially during the Depression. Still others turned to it when faced with dependent families, language barriers or simply the notion that women belonged in the home. Pura Belpré, writer and folklorist, recalls that Puerto Rican women sold their needlework from door to door during the thirties. One woman, Doña María, ran a household in *El Barrio* which included four children, elderly grandparents and a husband. Her major responsibilities, while the children were little and her husband worked in the cigar industry, lay in the home. There she made lampshades and other piecework items for several years, but as soon as her children were old enough she began working in a local factory, eventually becoming plant forelady.[3]

While salaries in general averaged about 21 dollars a week or less for Spanish-surnamed individuals before the Depression, salaries for piecework remained very low throughout the interwar years. During the thirties, furthermore, most Puerto Ricans who were employed earned wages below W.P.A. (Works Progress Administration) and Home Relief Bureau levels, and women were usually paid even less

(Chenault, 1970:69-88; Rubenstein, 1956). Piecework was considered among the lowest-paying occupations. Moreover, increasing restrictions placed on piecework by the New York State Department of Labor and the minimum-wage laws of the period failed to control the growing numbers of illegal business ventures. Employers paid little heed to minimum-wage requirements, especially since few Puerto Ricans knew their rights in this area (Chenault, 1970:76).

Few women complained about either the work or their low wages as pieceworkers. Perhaps because they failed to view their skills as valuable or because home work offered many advantages not readily available to those who worked outside the home, Puerto Rican pieceworkers seldom saw themselves as victims of exploitation. One interviewee emphasized the degree of independence possible when one was able to work at one's own pace. Doña Julia remembers:

> At that time (1937) I started to hem handkerchiefs in the house, while I awaited the birth of my first baby, to earn extra money. My husband worked for the W.P.A. three weeks out of every month earning 15 dollars a week. A Mexican lady had a small factory on Eighth Avenue and either me or my husband would go there to pick up packages of handkerchiefs once a week. I would work a little in the morning and at night. The rest of the time was devoted to housework, cooking and cleaning and that sort of thing. Later on, my time went to the baby.[4]

Although believed to have declined considerably by the thirties, home work continued well into the fifties, according to the women interviewed. Piecework in Puerto Rican households provided a setting for social interaction similar to the North American custom of holding quilting bees or sewing circles. Young and old, grandmothers, aunts, mothers and children all participated in this work process, transmitting needlecraft traditions from one generation to another in an almost exclusively feminine world. Moreover, working together in the home stimulated informational exchanges among adults while allowing children a glimpse into the adult work world. In spite of the tediousness and continued low pay, piecework continued to enjoy popularity among Puerto Rican women specifically because it enabled them to work in the home and supplement family income. It also often served as a training ground for those who would eventually work outside the home.

Childcare

As Puerto Ricans entrenched themselves in the various *colonias* throughout the city, other income-producing opportunities emerged, enabling home-bound women to secure supplementary or, in some cases, primary incomes for their families. Minding children and taking in lodgers represented two such opportunities. Although some women in New York could rely on the ready availability of grandmothers, aunts or godmothers to look after their families while they worked, others were forced to leave their children behind with relatives in Puerto Rico while they sought to secure a New York livelihood. For the most part, childcare responsibilities in the early communities remained within familial configurations whenever possible, with the care of the young often relegated to unemployed household members. But the average Puerto Rican household in New York City prior to the Second World War consisted of a nuclear family unit—father, mother and children, with lodgers (often males).

If, as the census of 1925 suggested, the bulk of the Puerto Rican residences in South Central Harlem fell into the categories of simple or nuclear family households, then the extended family, which had traditionally allowed women the freedom to work outside the home in Puerto Rico, was virtually non-existent in New York. Census figures revealed that nuclear families or simple families with lodgers outnumbered extended families, extended families with lodgers and multifamily dwellings during the twenties and thirties (New York State Manuscript Census, 1925). Therefore, in the relative absence of an extended or multi-family situation, coupled with limited bilingualbicultural daycare institutions, another system for reliable childcare became essential for Puerto Ricans.

Childcare tasks previously undertaken by relatives defaulted to friends and acquaintances outside the kinship network who provided the services in exchange for a set fee. A grass-roots system of daycare was born from the merger of working mothers, who could ill afford to lose job security or union benefits, and women who remained at home for any number of reasons. Working Puerto Rican mothers left their children in the care of friends or relatives; the arrangement basically consisted of bringing the child, food and additional clothing to the mother-substitute and collecting him after work.

Women who opened their home to care for children found this a worthwhile economic venture, often increasing family earnings.

During the twenties and thirties women paid two or three dollars weekly per child for daycare, but by 1948 fees paid in private homes ranged between 10 and 12 dollars per week, adding further to an already cumbersome financial burden. Almost all of the women interviewed placed their children in the homes of either friends or relatives at some time during their working lives, and this system continued to offer more advantages than established institutions. Doña Celina came to New York on the eve of the Second World War with her infant daughter, whom she left in her sister's care while she worked in a local factory. Five years later, the births of a son and daughter curtailed outside employment but permitted Doña Celina the opportunity to mind neighborhood children. This practice continued for 35 years. Without a husband and on public assistance during hard times, she nevertheless managed to raise her own three children on the unpredictable earnings from piecework, selling her own handicrafts and caring for other people's children.

Lodgers

As childcare provided supplementary income and strengthened bonds among New York Puerto Ricans, so did taking in lodgers. Census enumerations often designated Puerto Rican women as heads of households composed primarily of lodgers. Within the lodger groups many migrants sought accommodations in the homes of friends, relatives or hometown acquaintances, but married couples or family units also boarded with one another. Lodgers often came from the same hometown as the head of the household. Through friends and relatives, migrants quickly discovered where they could obtain lodgings, often before coming to New York. In some cases multifamily or extended family dwellings were classified as households with lodgers, since the census takers listed but one household head. In reality, several families shared living space and expenses equally. Doña Julia, for instance, recalls sharing an apartment with her husband and baby and her brother and his family during the Depression.

Sharing households either as lodgers or as heads of households with lodgers appeared to be a common experience among the women interviewed. Almost without exception those women who migrated from Puerto Rico lived in New York residences as lodgers while those who were born in New York related tales of woe regarding the not infrequent, unannounced arrival of some relative or hometown acquaintance. One woman stated, "We never knew when we left for school in the morning if our bedrooms would still be ours in the evening. Sleeping arrangements were in constant flux depending on how many people lived with us at any given time." As early as 1925, a full 24 percent of the 7,322 Spanish-surnamed inhabitants of South Central Harlem were classified as lodgers. Of these, males outnumbered females almost two to one. A plurality of this population, about 34 percent, was in the 15 to 25 age group, with a significant 26 percent grouped into the 26 through 35 age bracket (New York State Manuscript Census, 1925). The lodger group, therefore, was in its most productive work years, often single, and represented the future household heads of the Puerto Rican communities. One interviewee, Doña Rosa, was perhaps typical of most of the women lodgers of the period. She commented:

> I came to live in my step-sister's house in 1926, when I was about 20 years old. Quite a few of my cousins were already there with wives and children — all living in my step-sister's house on 116th Street and Park Avenue. The household consisted of about 15 people and each suitable bedroom was assigned to several of us. Most of us worked, except for my step-sister, who had youngsters, and her sister, who did all the cooking and cleaning for all of us. I started to work right away but never got used to the dirt and winter darkness of the city. I earned about 15 dollars weekly and paid six or seven dollars for my room out of that even though I hardly ever ate at the house. On my days off, I'd go visit other relatives in the city and usually ate with them.[5]

It was not unusual for women migrants to make the ocean crossing alone, since they were met, for the most part, by relatives who had either invited them to come or were prepared to assume responsibility for them once they arrived. Doña Clara, an interviewee who arrived almost a decade after Doña Rosa, recalls little change in the customs and practices of lodgers. Her experiences were similar to many others travelling the same road.

My brother sent for me, as he had been in New York several years, and we both lived with a cousin on 144th Street. New York didn't really seem too oppressive to me, perhaps because I arrived during the summer months and people socialized outdoors all of the time. Afterwards, I moved into the home of friends from my home town of Cabo Rojo and when my brother married, I was invited to live with them. I stayed in his home until I myself married. Then I moved to the West Side.[6]

Doña Perfecta, an early settler whose home was considered a New York stepping-stone by her brothers and sisters, believed lodgers played an important role in the survival of the early communities. In her opinion, they were valuable to the continuity of various communities because they kept open the networks of communication between the island and the New York enclaves. They also contributed to the support of the household, enabling women in particular, who carried the burden of providing room and board, to add to the family's income. Through ritual kinship (*compadrazgo*), lodgers expanded the familial system at a time when the Puerto Rican communities were most vulnerable both in size and in perpetuating their values and traditions.

The practice of taking in boarders based on the purchase of room, board and domestic services within an established household was not limited to Puerto Rican communities. Black Harlem settlements disclose the existence of enlarged households often containing kin and unmarried lodgers in the census records of 1915 and 1925. Similarly, lodgers resided in Jewish and Italian homes during the same period (Gutman, 1976; Howe, 1976). In general, the census records for East and South Central Harlem households convey a sense of community and mutual support among the many racial/ethnic groups inhabiting these areas, since Puerto Ricans were found living as lodgers in European or South American homes, while the latter occupied similar positions in Puerto Rican homes. However, after the thirties, when large numbers of Puerto Ricans resided in the city, ethnic mixtures within households appear to diminish.

Outside Work

Although most Puerto Rican women wage earners worked in their homes, close to 25 percent of those living in New York City participated in the labor force as cigar-makers and domestics, as typists and stenographers, in the needletrades industries as operatives and unskilled workers, in the laundries or restaurants and in the fields as agricultural workers. The first reports of female factory or field workers appeared in newspapers or government documents around the turn of the 20th century. Puerto Rican women were part and parcel of the migrant labor force contracted to work in various parts of the Western Hemisphere, in the process establishing communities in which cultural traditions and institutions resembled closely those in their native land.[7]

The decade of the twenties witnessd an increase in the number of Puerto Rican women working in New York factories. Skilled labor predominated in at least two industries traditionally associated with Puerto Ricans — the needletrades and cigar-making. Women were well represented in the cigar industry, not only among skilled and unskilled workers, but as readers in many of the New York factories.[8]

During the same period Spanish-language journals and newspapers vigorously advertised in their classified sections for both skilled and unskilled garment workers. Want ads frequently called for sewing-machine operators and workers in embroidery, crocheting and lace as pieceworkers in the home or in the factory. This advertising attracted the attention of job-seeking women. Of the 3,496 women listed in the four Assembly Districts of South Central Harlem, for example, 17 percent were involved in factory work of some sort, as operatives, dressmakers or seamstresses (New York State Manuscript Census, 1925).

In 1930, the Department of Labor of Puerto Rico established an employment service in response to the growing numbers of migrants living in New York City. This agency functioned also as liaison between the migrant communities and the larger non-Hispanic society, providing a wide range of social services as well as jobs. Located in the midst of the Hispanic community on 116th Street in Manhattan, about 3,600 women obtained job placements through this agency over a six-year period. Approximately 42 percent were employed as domestics, while needle workers, hand sewers and factory workers comprised an almost equal percentage. Of all the Puerto Rican women workers who applied to this agency, roughly 80 percent found work as operatives or in domestic services. Although jobs were at a premium during this period, the agency's activities indicate the type

65

of work available to Puerto Ricans, which continued to be concentrated in the blue-collar sector (Chenault, 1970: 73-75).

Migration and work by women did not produce major changes in their roles within Puerto Rican society, for the image of dutiful wives, loving mothers and respectful sisters and daughters remained paramount to their way of thinking. Neither did profound changes occur in the work world to which they were committed, since they neither demanded nor were given the opportunity to control strategic resources or educational facilities. Only a handful became factory foreladies or union representatives and fewer still owned their own businesses. In most fields of endeavor decision-making remained male-dominated and organizations continued to be male-oriented. Yet subtle messages were filtering down to younger generations: women were not only mothers and wives; women also worked and were involved.

NOTES

1. An extensive analysis of the 1925 New York State Manuscript Census was undertaken by the History Task Force of the Centro de Estudios Puertorriqueños, City University of New York. The author is a member of this task force.
2. See Fernández Cintrón and Quintero Rivera (1974). In addition, Angel Quintero Rivera has written on the role of the Puerto Rican labor force and articles have appeared on this topic in Claridad and several other Puerto Rican newspapers.
3. Interview with Maria Bonilla, New York City, Summer, 1976.
4. Taped interview with Julia Sánchez González, Río Piedras, Puerto Rico, Summer, 1977, edited and translated by the author.
5. Taped interview with Rosa Roma, Santurce, Puerto Rico, Summer, 1977, edited and translated by the author.
6. Taped interview with Clara Rodríguez, Cabo Rojo, Puerto Rico, Summer, 1977, edited and translated by the author.
7. See New York Times, "The Porto Rican exodus," April 4, 1901; and Centro de Estudios Puertorriqueños, 1976.
8. Readers were individuals hired to read in cigar factories. They would read aloud journals, newspapers, novels, magazines, and books with the purpose of informing and entertaining the workers. This practice was limited

to factories with Spanish-speaking workers. Readers were paid by donations from workers' salaries. For more information see César Andreu Iglesias (1977).

REFERENCES

Andreu Iglesias, César, ed. Memorias de Bernardo Vega. Río Piedras, P.R.: Ediciones Huracán. 1977.

Centro de Estudios Puertorriqueños. "Documentos de la Migración Puertorriqueña," No. 3. Unpublished manuscript. New York: CUNY Graduate Center. 1976.

Chenault, Lawrence R. The Puerto Rican Migrant in New York City. Second edition. New York: Russell and Russell. 1970.

Fernández Cintrón, Celia and Marcia Quintero Rivera. "Bases de la sociedad sexista en Puerto Rico." Revista/Review Interamericana 4, 2 (Summer). 1974.

Gutman, Herbert. The Black Family in Slavery and Freedom, 1750-1925. New York: Pantheon Press. 1976.

Howe, Irving. The World of Our Fathers. New York: Harcourt, Brace, Jovanovich. 1976.

New York State Manuscript Census. The New York State Manuscript Census, 1925. Assembly Districts 16, 17, 18, 19. New York City: Hall of Records, Municipal Building. 1925.

Rubenstein, Annette and Associates. I Vote My Conscience: Debates, Speeches and Writings of Vito Marcantonio, 1935-50. New York: The Marcantonio Memorial. 1956.

Senior, Clarence and Donald Watkins. "Toward a Balance Sheet of Puerto Rican Migration," in U.S. — Puerto Rico Commission on the Status of Puerto Rico, Status of Puerto Rico: Selected Background Studies. Washington, D.C.: U.S. Government Printing Office. 1966.

Smith, M. Estelle. "Networks and migration resettlement: Cherchez la femme." Anthropological Quarterly 49, 1 (January). 1976.

Work and Family: The Recent Struggle of Puerto Rican Females

Introduction

Why did the labor force participation of Puerto Rican women go from being the highest among women in New York in mid-century to the lowest in the 1970s (Ríos, 1985)? The Santana Cooney and Colón article was among the earliest to focus on this issue. They examined human capital dimensions, such as low skill levels and limited education among the women workers. Other analyses of labor force participation took this approach; however, Santana Cooney and Colón began to address dimensions that also compounded women's labor market situation, e.g., structural increases in service sector employment, rapidly changing computer and automation technology, and the flight of industry to sunbelt states and international sites. The authors speculated that the levels of labor force participation among Puerto Rican women, in a post-modern economy characterized by industrial decline, were influenced by a combination of factors.

Recent literature has continued this more broad-based approach and it has explored new dimensions that influence women and work. For example, fundamental issues that intersect transnationalism, capitalism, colonialism and global movements of workers are the focus of some of the research (Ortiz, N.D.). Current scholars also broach the topic from multiple and inter-related perspectives; from the unionization of women workers to the feminization of poverty and female headed-households.

WORK AND FAMILY:
THE RECENT STRUGGLE OF
PUERTO RICAN FEMALES

by Rosemary Santana Cooney and Alice Colón

Contrary to the overall optimistic outlook portrayed in several studies (Kantrowitz, 1968; Macisco, 1968; Fitzpatrick, 1968; Jaffe, et al., 1976), the relative economic position of the Puerto Rican community has deteriorated. At the national level and within New York City, findings have consistently indicated that while absolute median income of Puerto Rican families has improved between 1960 and 1970, the median income of Puerto Rican families relative to all families has declined (Puerto Rico Planning Board, 1972; Bureau of Labor Statistics, 1975; Wagenheim, 1975). The Puerto Rico Planning Board has argued that two major reasons for this relative decline were the rapid growth of female-headed families and the declining labor-force participation of Puerto Rican females.

The higher prevalence of poverty among Puerto Rican female-headed families as compared to husband/wife families has been well documented for 1970. This fact in conjunction with the increase in female-headed families within the Puerto Rican community leads to the argument that the deterioration in median family income for all Puerto Ricans is associated with the changing family structure. It has even been suggested, based on the experience of blacks at the national level and total families in New York City, that the relative income of

Dr. Rosemary Santana Cooney is Professor and Chair of the Department of Sociology, Fordham College at Rose Hill, Bronx, N.Y. **Dr. Alice Colón** is Director of Project CERES, Centro de estudios, recursos y servicios a la mujer, at the Center for Social Research, University of Puerto Rico, Rio Piedras, P.R. Research support provided by the National Institute of Mental Health and the Ford-Rockefeller Research Program on Population and Development Policy is greatfully acknowledged.

Puerto Rican husband/wife families may have improved while that of Puerto Rican female-headed families deteriorated.

· The low participation of Puerto Rican females in the labor force has also been extensively documented (Office of the President, 1973; Wagenheim, 1975; Bureau of Labor Statistics, 1975), both in comparison to blacks and whites and other Spanish-descent groups. With the exception of research focused on New York City, little attention has been directed toward the fact that Puerto Rican female participation has not always been low, but has been declining. This decline is important because the family income of both husband/wife and female-headed families is noticeably higher if the wife or female head is working.

Not only are both of these trends importantly related to the changing economic position of the Puerto Rican community, but they are also particularly critical in terms of their influence on the situation of Puerto Rican women. In a short paper it is impossible to do justice to the determinants and consequences of either of these important trends. Our purpose is more modest. We have been doing research on Puerto Rican female labor-force participation and Puerto Rican female-headed families, and we believe it is important to summarize our findings to date as well as to document carefully these trends within the Puerto Rican community in comparison with other racial/ethnic groups.

Declining Labor-Force Participation of Puerto Rican Females

Although there has been much research focused on female labor-force participation, it has been primarily concerned with the increasing integration of women, especially married women, into the work force. Studies have shown this trend to be true for white and black women. The decennial census data clearly show that other racial/ethnic groups have also participated in this trend. This makes the decline in Puerto Rican female labor-force participation very significant. Of the eight racial/ethnic groups shown in Table 1, only the Puerto Rican females have experienced a decline in participation, from 38.9 percent in 1950 to 36.3 percent in 1960 to a low of 29.8 percent in 1970. It is also important to notice that in 1950, the participation rate of Puerto Rican females was higher than both whites and blacks. In fact, only the

71

Japanese females had a higher rate than the Puerto Ricans in 1950. By 1970 the participation rate of Puerto Rican females was lower than all the other groups.

Table 1. Changes in Female Labor-Force Participation,[a] 1950-1970, for Racial/ Ethnic Groups

Racial/Ethnic Groups	1950	1960	1970	Absolute Change	Relative Percent Change
White[b]	28.1	33.6	38.9	+10.8	+38.4
Black	37.4	42.2	44.5	+7.1	+18.9
Mexican[c]	21.9	28.8	33.8	+11.9	+54.3
Puerto Rican	38.9	36.3	29.8	−9.1	−23.4
Japanese	44.6	44.1	47.6	+3.0	+6.7
Chinese	30.7	44.2	47.5	+16.8	+54.7
Filipino	24.0	36.2	52.6	+28.6	+119.2
Indian	17.0	25.5	33.1	+16.1	+94.7

[a] The participation rate is simply the percent of working-age females (14+ years) in the labor force.

[b] Total whites includes Spanish-heritage whites.

[c] The Spanish-surname population is used to identify this group in all three decades.

Source: 1950 Census of Population, Volume IV, Special Reports, Parts 3B, 3C, 3D; 1960 Census of Population, Special Reports, PC(2)-1B, PC(2)-1C, PC(2)-1D; 1970 Census of Population, Special Reports, PC(2)-1D, PC(2)-1E, PC(2)-1F, PC(2)-1G; 1970 Census of Population, U.S. Summary, Volume C.

Suggestive explanations for the low participation of Puerto Rican females have been offered in the literature. Several factors receiving repeated attention are: (1) the patriarchal family structure associated with the Spanish heritage; (2) the low education of Puerto Rican females; (3) the high fertility of Puerto Rican females; (4) the recency of Puerto Rican arrival in large numbers; and (5) the deteriorating job market for low-skilled workers. These factors are usually suggested within the context of explaining the present low participation of Puerto Rican females rather than the decline in their participation. In addition, these explanations are largely restricted to understanding the situation in New York City. In the following discussion, we attempt to evaluate the importance of these factors in explaining the decline in Puerto Rican female participation.

• The low participation rate of Puerto Rican females in 1970 has received wide publication partly because it is consistent with the explanation that traditional Hispanic family structure defines the woman's place as belonging in the home. Yet Mexican-American females, the largest female Spanish-language group in the United States, are increasingly integrated into the work force. More importantly, such a simplistic idea is not very helpful in explaining either the high Puerto Rican female participation in 1950 or the dramatic decline in their participation between 1950-1970.

In looking at the factors affecting Puerto Rican labor-force participation, it is important to examine not only national trends, but also regional differences, since regions differ not only in terms of labor-market conditions but also in terms of characteristics of the competing labor supply. We are particularly interested in whether the national decline in Puerto Rican female participation is also evident in different parts of the country or whether it is primarily a characteristic of the New York area where a majority of Puerto Ricans still live.

• In 1960, detailed data published on female labor-force participation by age for Puerto Ricans were available for New York, New Jersey, Illinois, and California, the four states with the largest numbers of Puerto Ricans. In 1970, these same four states still contained the largest concentrations of Puerto Ricans. Eighty-five and eighty-three percent of all Puerto Ricans living in the United States resided in one of these states in 1960 and 1970, respectively. The 1960-1970 decade is particularly relevant to the study of declining Puerto Rican female participation because the largest drop occurred in this decade.

Data on Puerto Rican female participation in 1960 and 1970 are shown in Table 2 separately by age for birth and parentage groups (first and second generation, respectively). Comparative data on total white females are also provided.

In all four states, the participation rate of white females increased, with a single exception. Thus the national trend of increasing white female participation is representative of changes occurring in New York, New Jersey, Illinois, and California for different age groups. The national trend of declining Puerto Rican female participation, however, is not representative of changes for Puerto Ricans in differ-

Table 2. Labor-Force Participation Rates for Puerto Rican and Total White Females by Age in Selected States, 1960-1970

	New York			New Jersey			Illinois			California		
	Puerto Rican		Total	Puerto Rican		Total	Puerto Rican		Total	Puerto Rican		Total
1960	Birth	Parentage	White	Birth	Parentage	White	Birth	Parentage	White	Birth	Parentage	White
14-19	25.0	24.3	26.5	24.3	21.0	26.1	26.5	14.0	30.0	21.4	15.1	23.3
20-24	47.2	54.3	52.0	41.6	46.2	50.9	39.8	33.0	47.4	47.9	33.9	44.1
25-34	40.8	42.0	34.3	39.2	31.6	32.0	37.0	30.7	33.2	39.0	38.4	36.1
35-44	45.9	49.0	41.5	42.7	52.1	40.9	38.2	41.2	42.1	43.1	41.7	44.4
45-64	34.3	39.3	43.7	29.6	41.2	41.9	20.7	29.4	43.6	35.8	36.6	43.6
1970												
14-19	17.1	16.8	25.5	25.4	15.7	28.2	28.4	18.7	32.3	23.7	17.9	25.2
20-24	32.4	48.1	57.6	41.1	55.3	60.3	48.3	49.6	59.2	56.0	62.7	57.1
25-34	24.1	33.7	39.8	33.0	40.2	38.3	37.9	43.5	42.3	45.0	49.6	45.9
35-44	31.3	43.5	46.6	45.2	46.5	47.5	45.7	46.8	49.2	50.2	47.4	50.0
45-64	31.4	44.2	50.2	32.8	b	50.4	30.1	58.5a	50.6	40.2	43.1	47.6

a The base number for this percentage is small by Census Bureau standards and should be interpreted cautiously.
b This percentage (70.5) is not consistent with the other data. Because we have been unable to determine why this value is so high, we have deleted it from the main body of the table.

Source: 1960 Census of Population, Subject Report. Puerto Ricans in the U.S. PC(2)-1D; 1970 Census of Population, Subject Report. Puerto Ricans in the U.S. PC(2)-1E; Volume 1, State Volumes.

ent parts of the country. In Illinois and California, the participation of Puerto Rican females has increased for every age group whether born in Puerto Rico or in the United States. Even in New Jersey, the picture predominantly is one of increasing participation—three of the nine age/parentage groups show a decline of 5-6 percentage points. On the other hand, only in New York is the trend dramatically downward for both first- and second-generation Puerto Rican females.

In 1960, Puerto Rican female participation rates in New York not only compared favorably with California, Illinois, and New Jersey, but often exceeded them. By 1970, the situation was reversed, with participation rates for age/generation groups in New York being predominantly lower than in California, Illinois, and New Jersey. The national trend of declining Puerto Rican female participation is critically related to the situation of Puerto Ricans in New York, partly because of the large numbers of Puerto Ricans living there, but also because the decline in female participation was so dramatic, especially among the large group of Puerto Rican birth.

In the two studies summarized below, systematic attention was directed toward assessing the relative importance of individual characteristics as compared to structural characteristics. At the aggregate level, we studied the influence of labor-market conditions, socioeconomic characteristics of the Puerto Rican female labor supply, and assimilation factors on variations in Puerto Rican female participation rates among 56 cities in New York, New Jersey, and Pennsylvania (Cooney, 1979). The analysis clearly showed the importance of labor-market conditions (demand for operative workers, industry mix, the unemployment rate, median female earnings). The overall net effect of socioeconomic characteristics of Puerto Rican females, including education and fertility, as well as the net effect of assimilation variables, including percent first generation and percent recent migrants among Puerto Rican females, was small and insignificant. In other words, favorable labor-market conditions, especially a high demand for operative workers, provided work opportunities to which Puerto Rican females *did* respond. Study of factors affecting the participation of individual Puerto Rican females must proceed with an awareness of the importance of these larger structural factors.

Because the national decline in Puerto Rican female participation is critically related to the large numbers of Puerto Ricans still living within the depressed New York labor market, we did a further study comparing individual Puerto Rican females with whites in the New York metropolitan area (Cooney and Warren, 1977).[1] We did find that the participation rates of individual Puerto Rican and white females were affected by such socioeconomic characteristics as age, education, number of children, and presence of children under six. The education and fertility variables were major factors in explaining the difference between white and Puerto Rican participation in 1970. However, these socioeconomic variables did not help us in explaining why Puerto Rican female participation was declining. In spite of higher educational achievement and lower fertility of Puerto Ricans in 1970 as compared to 1960, the participation of Puerto Rican females declined from 38.6 to 29.2. While we only had limited information on assimilation factors at this level, we did not find our birth/migration variable to be a significant factor in either 1960 or 1970.[2]

Changes in demand for female labor by skill levels were dramatic and favored the more educated groups in the New York metropolitan area. Even though the Puerto Rican female sample had improved their education in the past decade, these changes were slow compared to the dramatic shift in demand for highly-educated female labor. Moreover, the loss of low-skilled jobs has disproportionately affected Puerto Rican females, while the expansion of higher skilled jobs has favored whites. The competitive advantage of whites may partially explain why many better-educated Puerto Rican females are leaving New York state for other parts of the United States.

The question of why Puerto Rican female participation has declined is far from being fully answered. Our research has shown that individualistic explanations offered for the low rate of Puerto Rican female participation are not very useful in explaining why their participation has declined. In particular, individual characteristics such as education, fertility, and recency of migration were not significant factors explaining variations in Puerto Rican female participation either among cities or among individual Puerto Rican females in the New York metropolitan area between 1960 and 1970. In contrast, unfavorable labor-market conditions and large declines in central-city industries in which Puerto Ricans are concentrated are part of the answer.

Growth of Puerto Rican Female-Headed Families

Because female-headed families are largely poverty families, the rapid growth of such families has important implications for the overall economic well being of the Puerto Rican community. These implications may even extend beyond the present situation to the future economic well being of the Puerto Ricans to the extent that larger proportions of young Puerto Rican children are raised in poor female-headed households. The growth of female-headed families is not unique to the Puerto Rican community, but reflects a national trend. What makes this growth distressing is that the rate of increase of female-headed families within the Puerto Rican community is so high — surpassing not only the national trend but also the rate of increase within the black community.

Published data on the family structure of the major census-identified racial/ethnic groups are only available for 1960 and 1970. In 1960, 15.3 percent of all Puerto Rican families were headed by females (Table 3). By 1970, this percent had increased to 24.1. In 1970, in the Middle Atlantic region (New York, New Jersey, and Pennsylvania), where 77 percent of Puerto Ricans resided, the percent of all Puerto Rican families headed by a female was 28. Among blacks and whites, the comparable figures are 32 and 9 percent (see Table 4). The number of Puerto Rican female-headed families within the Middle Atlantic region has increased by 158 percent. If we focus on female-headed families with own children under 18 years in the home, the increase is even larger: 216 percent.

Whether one looks at this absolute percent increase or the percent change in the total number of female-headed families, the growth of Puerto Rican female-headed families is much greater than among other racial/ethnic groups and between two and three times the increase among black families.[3] In the Middle Atlantic region, the absolute growth of Puerto Rican female-headed families is five times the increase among whites. The family structure of Puerto Ricans is *not* becoming more similar to the majority white population, but, on the contrary, is becoming more similar to the historically disadvantaged black minority population.

Table 3. Changes in the Proportion and Number of Female-Headed Families by Racial/Ethnic Group, 1960-1970

Racial/ Ethnic Group	Percent of All Families Headed by Females		Absolute Percent Change	Relative Change in Number of Female-Headed Families[a]
	1960	1970		
White[b]	8.1	9.0	+ .9	+25.2
Black	21.7	27.4	+5.7	+55.6
Mexican[c]	11.9	13.4	+1.5	+57.4
Puerto Rican	15.3	24.1	+8.8	+161.5
Japanese	7.8	10.3	+2.5	+77.7
Chinese	6.1	6.7	+ .6	+112.1
Filipino	5.4	8.6	+3.2	+217.9
Indian	16.4	18.4	+2.0	+85.3

[a] Expressed as a percent.
[b] Total whites includes Spanish-heritage whites.
[c] The Spanish-surname population is used to identify this group in both decades.
Source: See Table 1; 1960 Census of Population, Special Report, Families PC(2)-4A.

Table 4. Growth of Female-Headed Families Compared to Husband/Wife Families by Racial/Ethnic Group, Middle Atlantic Region, 1960-1970

	Puerto Rican	Black[a]	White[a]
Female-Headed Families as Percent of All Families			
1960	17.7	24.2	7.5
1970	28.0	32.1	9.1
Relative Change in Number by Family Type			
Husband/Wife	+45.0	+29.0	+ 6.8
Female-Headed	+158.0	+93.9	+31.4
Relative Change in Number by Family Type with Own Children under 18			
Husband/Wife	+52.7	+35.3	−6.9
Female-Headed	+216.0	+130.3	+48.2

[a] See Note 1.
Source: 1960 and 1970 public-use sample tapes from the decennial censuses.

In the literature concerned with the growth of female-headed families, two factors have received a good deal of attention — rising marital instability and changes in living arrangements. The first is self-evident; the latter refers to the increased likelihood that maritally-disrupted mothers will set up their own household rather than live with their parents or other relatives. In particular, a favorite argument is that the increasing availabilty of welfare encourages marital disruption and allows the mother to set up her own household. Additionally, when focusing on the growth of female-headed families among Puerto Ricans and blacks, it has been suggested that large numbers of Puerto Rican and black female family heads are migrating to the Middle Atlantic region because of high welfare benefits.

In a study of demographic components of the growth in the number of female-headed families, marital disruption was found to be the major factor explaining the growth of white female-headed families, but not of Puerto Rican or black female-headed families (Cooney, 1977). There is both a larger number of maritally-disrupted Puerto Rican and black women in 1970 than in 1960 and a larger number of Puerto Rican and black disrupted mothers setting up their own household in 1970 as compared to 1960. But the proportion of maritally-disrupted females relative to all ever-married women, and the proportion of disrupted mothers heading their own household to all disrupted mothers, has changed very little during the decade for Puerto Ricans and blacks. That migration is not a major factor is suggested by the finding that migrants in the 1965 to 1970 period make up only a small percent of all female-headed families — six percent of all Puerto Rican female-headed families and nine percent of all black female-headed families. Two factors that are relatively important in explaining the increase in the absolute number of Puerto Rican and black female family heads are: (1) the larger numbers of Puerto Rican and black women, due to population growth, exposed to the risk of being a female head of family in 1970 than in 1960; and (2) maritally-disrupted Puerto Rican and black women in 1970 were more likely to have children in the home than in 1960.

The rapid growth of female-headed families is of great concern because of the high incidence of poverty. To appreciate the magnitude of the problem, we now turn our attention to changes in median family income for husband/wife and female-headed families between 1960 and 1970 separately for Puerto Rican, black, and white families (see Table

5). National comparisons of income would be misleading because of great regional differences in the cost of living. Therefore, we narrowed our focus in the income analysis which follows to the Middle Atlantic region (New York, New Jersey, Pennsylvania).

Table 5. Median Family Income by Family Type for Racial/Ethnic Groups, Middle Atlantic Region, 1960-1970

	Puerto Rican	Black[a]	White[a]
Median Family Income for Each Group			
1960			
Husband/Wife	$4,050	$4,830	$ 6,555
Female-Head	$2,710	$2,760	$ 3,826
Female-Head Income as Percent of Husband/Wife Income	66.9	57.1	58.4
1970			
Husband/Wife	$6,880	$9,030	$11,421
Female Head	$3,260	$4,070	$ 7,549
Female Head Income as Percent of Husband/Wife Income	47.4	45.1	66.1
Median Family Income of Groups as Percent of White Husband/Wife Family Income			
1960			
Husband/Wife	61.8	73.7	100.0
Female Head	41.3	42.1	58.4
1970			
Husband/Wife	60.2	79.1	100.0
Female Head	28.5	35.6	66.1

[a]See Note 1.
Source: See Table 4.

In both 1960 and 1970, the median family income of female-headed families is considerably lower than the median income of husband/wife families. Within racial/ethnic groups, the income of female-headed families is only 57-67 percent of husband/wife family income. The

80

relative income position of white female-headed families is more favorable than black female-headed families, with Puerto Rican female-headed families being in the worst position. Even more importantly, the relative position of Puerto Rican and black female-headed families compared to husband/wife families has deteriorated over the decade, while the relative position of white female-headed families *has improved*.

It is important to make absolute comparisons among racial/ethnic groups. To facilitate this, we have taken the high income of white husband/wife families as the standard and expressed the income of the other groups as a percent of this standard. Although the median income of Puerto Rican husband/wife families did not improve relative to changes in white husband/wife income, it did *keep up* with the substantial increases in income of white husband/wife families. In other words, the median family income of Puerto Rican husband/wife families did not deteriorate over the decade. The often-noted *increasing* gap between Puerto Rican family income and total family income is related to the deteriorating economic situation of Puerto Rican female-headed families and to their rapid growth within the Puerto Rican community. When we restrict our attention to Puerto Rican husband/wife families the outlook is not quite so bleak.

While Puerto Rican husband/wife families have only managed to keep stride with changes in income, black husband/wife families have improved their relative income position. Moreover, in 1970, the median income for black husband/wife families was 79 percent of white husband/wife families while the income of Puerto Rican husband/wife families was only 60 percent.

It is also important to note that the economic disadvantage of female-headed families would be greater for all three racial/ethnic groups if we had focused our attention only on female-headed families with children under 18 in the household. But even within this group of female-headed families, whites *improved* their relative income position, while the relative income of Puerto Rican and black families *declined*.

Thus far we have separated our discussion of Puerto Rican female labor-force participation from our discussion of the growth of female-headed families. Yet, these two processes are not independent of one another. We found in our intercity analyses of Puerto Rican female participation rates that the most important socioeconomic characteristic of Puerto Rican females affecting their participation was not our indicator of Puerto Rican fertility or education, but the proportion of Puerto Rican females heading families. From previous research on women in the labor force, we know that female heads generally have higher rates of participation than female nonheads of households (usually wives). Yet our results showed a strong negative relationship, that is, cities with a higher proportion of Puerto Rican females heading families had lower rates of Puerto Rican female participation.

When we looked at the data for individual Puerto Rican females in the New York metropolitan area, we found that in 1960, the participation of Puerto Rican female heads was noticeably higher than nonheads (52.8 as compared to 34.9). But by 1970, these differences had disappeared, with Puerto Rican female heads having a participation rate of 28.4 and Puerto Rican female nonheads 29.5. Even after adjusting for other factors such as fertility, education, and age, the participation rates were very similar. What these analyses show is that the decline in Puerto Rican female participation was slight for Puerto Rican females who were not household heads, while the decline among female heads was a dramatic −24.4 percentage points. This pattern is also evident when the comparison is only between wives and female heads, both of whom have own children under 18 years in the household. The participation rate of these wives was stable from 1960 to 1970 while the participation of female family heads with children declined dramatically. Certainly an important factor related to the decreases in Puerto Rican labor-force participation in the New York area is the growth of female-headed families. In other words, the drop in Puerto Rican female participation is related to the dramatic decline in participation among Puerto Rican female family heads. The participation of nonheads and wives has remained relatively stable.

We have already referred to the deteriorating economic opportunities for Puerto Rican women with low education. These data suggest that this decline in job opportunities affected the participation of Puerto Rican female family heads more than Puerto Rican wives. Female family heads with children have an alternative to low-paying jobs that wives with children do not have — welfare. Durbin (1975) has documented the monetary attractiveness of welfare payments compared to the income from minimum-wage jobs in New York City. The inter-relationship of welfare, labor-force status, and family structure among Puerto Ricans deserves further careful study.

Overview

⋆ The relative economic position of Puerto Ricans, instead of improving as expected by many scholars, has deteriorated. We have seen that part of the explanation of this situation lies in the declining labor-force participation of Puerto Rican women and particularly in the deteriorating economic situation of Puerto Rican female heads of family. These trends cannot be explained by the characteristics of new migrants, although recent migrants may be reinforcing them. The evidence we have presented suggests that the migrant status of Puerto Rican women does not explain their labor-force participation and that only a small proportion of female family heads are recent migrants from the island.

We have suggested that changes in the industrial and occupational structure of the New York region have resulted in an upgrading of work-related educational requirements to which Puerto Rican women were not prepared to respond. Here is a group that alerts us to the fact that the optimistic vision of the integration of women into the market economy is limited to women of specific skill levels. It shows the precarious situation of women of lower skill levels who have been displaced from the labor force by present industrial changes.

Although Puerto Rican husband/wife families have not been able to improve their relative income position, these families were able to keep up with the substantial income increases experienced by white husband/wife families during the decade. This is significant given the fact that white wives increased their labor-force participation, while Puerto Rican wives' labor-force participation remained stable. It is necessary to study further the educational and occupational composition of Puerto Rican and white husband/wife families and their resulting income levels in 1960 and in 1970 to understand the factors related to the Puerto Rican—white income ratio. The median income of Puerto Rican husband/wife families in 1970 may be affected by a group of higher status husbands and wives who have much higher income than those at the bottom of the income distribution. In other words, the industrial changes during the 1960-1970 decade may have resulted in a cleavage between lower status and higher status Puerto Ricans. This cleavage may not be apparent in the median family income ratios that have been presented.

The cleavage within the Puerto Rican community is clear, however, between Puerto Rican female-headed families and husband/wife families. The maintenance of the relative position of Puerto Rican husband/wife families has been accompanied by the increasing deterioration of the income of families headed by Puerto Rican women. In 1960, it was this group of women who, having to fulfill the role of primary breadwinner, responded actively to the demand for low-skilled labor. It is their situation in 1970 which best portrays the effect of low-skill job displacement associated with the changing industrial structure. The participation of Puerto Rican female family heads declined dramatically during the decade. The availability of welfare benefits that match the earnings of low skill-level jobs is a factor to consider in the labor supplied by Puerto Rican female heads. It is within the context of job displacement, however, that the response of Puerto Rican women to work and welfare opportunities must be analyzed.

NOTES

1. Unless otherwise noted, the original research reported in the present paper uses the term "white" (or "black") to refer to persons in either of these two categories who were born in the U.S. and who are not Hispanic (i.e., not of Mexican, Puerto Rican, Cuban, Central or South American, or other Spanish origin or descent).

2. The categories for the birth/migration variable were: (1) born in Puerto Rico, migrated more than five years ago, (2) born in Puerto Rico, migrated within the last five years, and (3) born in the United States.

3. Filipinos have a higher relative increase, but the absolute percent of female-headed families is very small.

REFERENCES

Bureau of Labor Statistics. A Socio-Economic Profile of Puerto Rican New Yorkers. Regional Report 46. New York: Middle Atlantic Regional Office. 1975.

Cooney, Rosemary Santana. "Demographic components of growth in white, black and Puerto Rican female-headed families by stage of life cycle." Paper presented at the Southern Regional Demographic Group meeting, October. 1977.

"Intercity variations in Puerto Rican female participation," Journal of Human Resources, 14 (Spring): 222-235. 1979.

Cooney, Rosemary Santana and Alice Colón Warren. "Declining female participation among Puerto Rican New Yorkers: A comparison with native nonspanish white New Yorkers." Paper presented at the American Sociological Association meeting, September. Forthcoming in Ethnicity. 1977.

Durbin, Elizabeth. "The vicious cycle of welfare: Problems of the female headed household in New York City," in Cynthia B. Lloyd (ed.), Sex, Discrimination and the Division of Labor. New York: Columbia University Press. 1975.

Fitzpatrick, Joseph P. "Puerto Ricans in perspective: The meaning of migration to the mainland." International Migration Review 2 (Spring): 7-20. 1968.

Hanrieder, Barbara and Richard Mittenthal. Families Headed by Women in New York City. New York: Community Council of Greater New York. 1975.

Jaffe, A.J., Ruth M. Cullen and Thomas D. Boswell. Spanish Americans in the United States — Changing Demographic Characteristics. New York: Research Institute for the Study of Man. 1976.

Kantrowitz, Nathan. "Social mobility of Puerto Ricans: Education, occupation, and income changes among children of migrants, New York, 1950-1960." International Migration Review 2 (Spring): 53-72. 1968.

Macisco, John J. "Assimilation of Puerto Ricans on the mainland: A sociodemographic approach." International Migration Review 2 (Spring): 21-39. 1968.

Office of the President. Manpower Report of the President. Washington, D.C.: U.S. Government Printing Office. 1973.

Puerto Rico Planning Board. Puerto Rican Migrants: A Socio-Economic Study. Puerto Rico: Bureau of Social Planning. 1972.

Wagenheim, Kal. A Survey of Puerto Ricans on the U.S. Mainland in the 1970s. New York: Praeger. 1975.

Wilber, George L., Daniel E. Jaco, Robert J. Hagan, and Alfonso C. del Fierro, Jr. Spanish Americans and Indians in the Labor Market. Vol. II. Lexington, Kentucky: Social Welfare Research Institute. 1975.

Latin Music:
The Perseverance of a Culture

Introduction

Max Salazár's article is one of the earliest descriptions of the historical evolution of what is today a critically important dimension of the Puerto Rican and Latino experience: Latin music. At the time of his writing, however, Latin music had not yet been acknowledged in the way in which it is today. International recognition was yet to flower. Puerto Ricans and other Latinos in the barrios of the United States had been the major advocates and consumers of the music. The music had begun to create worldwide interest and curiosity, but the academic community had yet to discover it.

As we view this article today, we see how Latin music has grown into what is today internationally recognized as "Salsa." Salsa has been exported to, and further developed in, Latin America, Europe, and Japan—even South Africa has African salsa. As Dr. Felix Padilla (1990:98) notes, "As a Puerto Rican ethnic style, Salsa music grew very quickly in popularity." He argues that in the seventies a commercially-driven process was undertaken to incorporate Salsa into the popular cultures of other Spanish-speaking people. The effects in Latin America of the "Latinizing" of salsa is described by Calvo Ospina (1995). Today, there is house salsa, rap-salsa, cuatro-salsa, and the Orquesta de la Luz (which consists entirely of Japanese musicians) comes to New York City (the start of it all) to perform at Latino and non-Latino clubs. *The 1994-95 Salsa Club Directory* lists clubs and radio stations that span the perimeter of the United States (Zitko and Collins, 1994).

Salazár's article was also important then because it clarified (1) that Latin music existed and evolved from the earliest days of the Puerto Rican community in New York; (2) that Puerto Ricans were full participants in this evolution; (3) that its evolution depended on the interweaving of diverse strands of musical heritages. These "facts" have come to be accepted as part of the musical lore of today, but at the time of his writing, they were known only to a few. Salazár's article helped establish a history of artistic and cultural development, and this was reflected in the evolution and development of its music. His article also made clear the struggle of musicians and the exploitation and racism they experienced during this evolution.

Today, as we reflect on this article, we see not just that the Puerto Rican culture continues to persevere and grow through Latin music, but that other cultures do so as well. Salazár reminds us of the enormous debt we owe to those who have insisted on, and persisted, in the accurate and equitable documentation of our history.

LATIN MUSIC:
THE PERSEVERENCE OF A CULTURE

by Max Salazár

After 1917, when the Puerto Rican community in New York began to build itself with additional migrants, the stirrings of a Latin music scene emerged. In these early years of the community's existence, the works most often heard were *danzas* and *danzones*, traditional melodic songs which originated in the Caribbean. The South American *tangos* and the *boleros* were also common to the ears of the listening, dancing early Puerto Rican settlements. During the mid-1920's, there was one orchestra in New York City that played Latin music; it was directed by Vicente Sigler, a Cuban mulatto. Sigler, however, did not work in the Spanish-speaking community. His dances were held at the plush midtown hotels which were always packed.

Rafael Hernández

Rafael Hernández, acclaimed as Puerto Rico's most famous composer, lived in Cuba before relocating to Spanish Harlem in 1928. Here he wrote some of the Puerto Rican favorites that still stir the emotions with their melodic phrases and beautiful lyrics. Hernández opened *Almacenes Hernández*, the first Latin record store in East Harlem. It was located on the west side of Madison Avenue between 113th and 114th Streets. In the back of his store there was a piano on which his sister Victoria taught aspiring musicians. Every time a student came for a lesson she would chase Rafael out of the rocking

Mr. Max Salazár is a noted musicologist, author, historian and expert on Latin Music, based in New York. This paper was originally delivered as a lecture to a group of Puerto Rican Studies students at Lehman College, Bronx, N.Y.

chair near the piano where he was singing and strumming his guitar. Rafael would then take his instrument and a tin can of black coffee out onto the sidewalk and sit down near the edge of the curb with his feet in the gutter. There he would tune his guitar, write some lyrics on a piece of paper and begin to sing.

The melodic compositions and lyrical phrases which came from Hernández' heart exuded feelings of longing or loneliness, as if the man was remote from someone or something he loved deeply. It seemed as if the only way he could express his pangs of love was through the guitar he held in his left arm while his fingers searched the strings for the appropriate notes. The lyrics of *"Los Carreteros"* and *"Lamento Borincano"* indicate that the author's melancholia focused on the scenery, the folkways and people, the unique country-side aromas and the cuisine of an island in the Caribbean — Puerto Rico. While singing and playing his guitar, Hernández appeared to transport himself vicariously to his beloved Puerto Rico, leaving behind the cold concreteness of East Harlem. *"Lamento Borincano,"* perhaps the most popular of all Hernández's compositions, was written on the sidewalk in front of *Almacenes Hernández* in 1929.

During the same year, just before the stock market crash, Cuban bandleader Don Aspiazu visited New York to play the RKO Palace Theatre at Broadway and 46th Street. His interpretation of the tune, *"El Manisero"* (the Peanut Vendor), made him and his vocalist, Antonio Machín, the talk of the Latin communities. This song is classified as a *pregón*, a street vendor's cry, but it was played in the rhythm of *el son*. *El son* was invented during the turn of the century in Cuba and it has evolved to what we now term *el son Montuno*. *El son* was rhythmically overwhelming. During the late 20's this music overcame the popularity of the Argentinian *tango* popularized by vocalist Carlos Gardel.

El Teatro San José

By 1930, the livelihoods of Puerto Ricans had not yet improved in New York City. Puerto Ricans were employed in every menial job this city had to offer. Only a few educated, bilingual Puerto Ricans earned decent salaries, although some Puerto Ricans had already banded together politically. They vociferously protested their absence in civil service jobs and in other employment areas which provided good salaries. One Puerto Rican civic group in East Harlem promoted a dance to raise funds. A spokesman for the group approached the proprietress of the Park Palace Jewish Caterers, located at 110th Street and 5th Avenue, and rented the hall for a Saturday night. The dance was a financial success and inspired others to open their own entertainment establishments. Through the development of theatres, dance halls and record shops which opened for business throughout East Harlem, the Puerto Rican presence in the community became more visible. The Photoplay Theatre at 110th Street and 5th Avenue became *El Teatro San José*. In addition to showing Spanish-language motion pictures, it utilized local talent for its stage shows. Many vocalists, dancers and musicians who started their careers on the stage of *El San José* eventually gained national prominence.

Although many factors influenced the development of businesses catering to Latin tastes, the early success of Puerto Rican-sponsored Latin dances is recalled as a pivotal point in this development. The birth of organizations at a time of severe economic depression parallels the recent boom in Latin social clubs, after-hours places, and similar establishments in New York. There is a loose correlation between hard times and the expansion of social activity, particularly in the music and dance spheres. Thus, music continues to serve as an alternative to misery, as a support system for survival during difficult times.

The Spanish Music Center

In 1934, Gabriel Oller, a Puerto Rican, opened the Spanish Music Center, a store next to *El Teatro San José*. Besides selling RCA, Columbia, and Decca recordings, he sold pianola rolls and guitars. Unable to compete with *Almacenes Hernández*, he decided on a gimmick to attract customers. He founded the first Puerto Rican-owned recording company, the Dynasonic label, and he recorded in the back of his store. The recording studio was a medium-sized room that housed the necessary equipment. Oller recorded the music of the neighborhood trios and quartets. No matter how many musicians soloed, each one had to step up to the one microphone. Each musician received $3.00 for the session. The recordings were done on an acetate which was a test recording. Masters were made from the acetates. As the music was being recorded, one could see the acetate record spinning on the turntable while its needle cut into the acetate like a lathe machine. Long strands of acetate fibers fell to the floor. Business always picked up prior to the Christmas holidays, when Puerto Ricans bought every available *aguinaldo* recording.

The industry grew along with the interest in Latin music. Latin rhythms became a means of temporary escape from the daily problems, an indispensible crutch for determined Puerto Rican survival in an alien city. One always knew which Puerto Rican families had good incomes because one or more family members were musicians. Music provided the means to earn a few more dollars to supplement the primary income. The poor families who could not rent a hall for a wedding, a baptismal or a birthday party, held them in their own apartments. Unemployed Puerto Ricans raised rent and food money by holding dances in their apartments and charging the dancers a 25-cent fee. The musicians were paid with the money earned from the sale of beer, *maví, pasteles, alcapúrrias* or *pastelillos*.

During the 1930's a house party in *El Barrio* was an event. The apartment and hallway reeked with the spicy aroma of garlic and oregano, which emanated from the fresh hams in the oven. Thin slabs of *pernil* accompanied plates of steaming *arroz con gandules*. The elders drank beer that flowed from a wooden keg kept in the kitchen sink on top of a 25-cent block of ice. The bathtub, filled with cracked ice, covered the several flavors of soda pop the children drank. Trios or quartets, which consisted of a lead vocalist, a *maraca* player, a guitarist and sometimes a trumpeter, provided live music in the living room. They had the dancers swaying to romantic *boleros* and swinging to the rhythms of *el son, la guaracha* and the Puerto Rican *bombas* and *danzas*. As the evening came to a close each musician was $3.00 richer.

Club Kubanacán and Teatro Campoamor

Despite the growing numbers of proficient musicians, English-language stations refused to air Latin music, insisting there was no market for it. In 1934, Marcial Flores, a wealthy Puerto Rican, opened *El Club Kubanacán* at 114th Street and Lenox Avenue, hiring the house band of Afro-Cuban bandleader, Alberto Socarrás. Months later Flores rented the empty Mount Morris Theatre at 116th Street and 5th Avenue which he reopened as *El Teatro Campoamor*, where Socarrás' band also provided live entertainment. For the latter half of 1934, Hispanic New Yorkers were treated to Afro-Cuban music every evening between 10-10:30 p.m. and 3-3:30 a.m. over radio station WMCA. The music was broadcast from *El Kubanacán*.

In early 1935, vocalist Davilita and trumpeter Augusto Coen, two Puerto Rican musicians, left Socarrás' band to form a group under Coen's direction. Pianist Noro Morales, who had just arrived in New York from Puerta de Tierra, Puerto Rico, also joined the newly-formed band. Fernando Luis, a dance-promoter of Puerto Rican descent, convinced Socarrás and Coen that a musical "battle" between them would pack a dancehall. They agreed. The following day, each time the movie ended at *El Campoamor*, messages flashed across the screen: "FLASH! FLASH! FLASH! WAR! WAR! WAR! . . . BETWEEN CUBA AND PUERTO RICO . . . AT THE PARK PALACE LOCATED AT 110th STREET AND 5th AVENUE BETWEEN ALBERTO SOCARRAS OF CUBA AND AUGUSTO COEN OF PUERTO RICO." The financial success of this enterprise paved the way for more musical battles between Cuban and Puerto Rican musicians and ethnic pride urged dancers to support their compatriots.

Xavier Cugat and Machito

By the beginning of 1940, Latin music was still restricted largely to Spanish-speaking communities. A coast-to-coast musical composers' strike against radio networks by ASCAP (The American Society of Composers, Authors and Publishers) inadvertently enabled Latin music to free itself of restrictions. Radio networks were earning millions of dollars and ASCAP wanted a fair return of the royalties, since music was the main attraction. The public, deprived of all music, exhibited a willingness to listen to any kind of music. MCA (the Music Corporation of Artists) sold its recordings to the radio network. Among MCA's artists was Xavier Cugat, a Latin bandleader born in Spain. His recordings received coast-to-coast exposure, enabling Cugat to open doors for other Latin bandleaders.

The Machito orchestra, which was formed in December of 1940, became the first Latin orchestra to play the prominent midtown night clubs and stage shows. While World War II raged in the Far East and Europe, the orchestras of Machito, Enric Madriguerra, Marcelino Guerra, Miguelito Valdés, Noro Morales, Alberto Iznaga and Xavier Cugat grew in popularity. After the war, musicians Tito Puente, René Hernández and Joe Loco were gaining recognition as Latin music's best composers and arrangers. Vocalists Tito Rodríguez, Bobby Escoto and Vitín Avilés were always in demand. The popularity of the Cuban *mambo* in 1949 started a new trend in Latin music. The handful of popular bands at the time included Pérez Prado, Antonio Arcano and Arsenio Rodríguez. The two new additions were Tito Rodríguez and Tito Puente. The 1949 recordings of Machito's *"Asia Minor"* and Puente's *"Abaniquito"* provided the catalysts that brought most of this city's ethnic groups together musically. Overwhelmed by the Afro-Cuban *mambo* and the introduction of the *cha-cha-chá* in the early fifties, the Anglo community responded to and supported the organization of more Latin bands.

Several years passed before the Dominican Republic's favorite rhythm, *el merengue*, became popular among Hispanics and non-Hispanics alike. A few *merengue* bands were formed and a few were imported, but the ones heard most often were those of Don Santiago, Dioris Valladares and Angel Villorias' *"Conjunto Típico Cibaeño."* To further complicate matters, the following year Puerto Rican bandleader Rafael Cortijo popularized two of the island's folkloric rhythms, *la bomba* and *la plena*. *"Las Ingratitudes," "Mi Compay Chipuco"* and *"Máquina Landera," bomba* recordings of Ismael Rivera, became smash hits on the Seeco label. The already overcrowded field of Latin music now contended with bandleaders César Concepción, Joe Valle, Carlos Pizarro, Yayo El Indio, Moncho Leña and Mon Rivera, all specialists in the then-popular Puerto Rican rhythms.

The *pachanga* rhythm gained popularity in the early sixties when Charlie Palmieri, a Puerto Rican bandleader-pianist, introduced his arrangement, called a *charanga*. There were now over 100 Latin bands looking for work, as compared to less then 20 in 1949. Too many good bands and not enough places which paid top dollar was the scenario in 1962 when the issue of top billing surfaced.

Tito Puente and Eddie Palmieri

Top billing indeed determined who was going to earn the most money, and as the eye skimmed down the popularity list of names, the fees kept diminishing. With growing awareness among Latin musicians of the importance of billing, good will among musicians became a thing of the past. The history of the Latin music business in recent decades is rife with petty jealousies, envy, unfounded gossip and corruption. Fierce competition is evident even in the titles assumed by various groups. There is a "King of Latin Music" (Tito Puente), whose regal title suggests he is so good that he rules the domain. Not to be outdone, pianist-bandleader Eddie Palmieri, an extremely talented musician, has dubbed himself "The Sun of Latin Music," becoming Tito Puente's chief antagonist in the process.

Although the Latin music industry in New York City generates millions of dollars a year in record sales, the chief beneficiaries are the record-company owners, who control the music and the publishing rights. Composers who want exposure reluctantly give up their rights to the publisher in order to have their music recorded. Disc jockeys favor the most powerful record companies and play their records most often. Therefore, whoever is not under contract to a powerful company has little if any chance at all to survive. Latin bandleaders never receive the royalties due them from their hit recordings. Latin musicians rarely receive union-scale wages for recordings and club dates. Presently, Tito Puente, the all-time great and gifted musician, directs the hottest Latin orchestra in the United States and his band works three nights a week, sometimes four. Other Latin bands work once a week, once a month or once every two months.

Because of this situation, my advice is that you should learn to sing . . . learn to play a guitar, a trumpet or a saxophone, but consider carefully a musical career as your livelihood. If the attraction to Latin music is compelling, perhaps it should become a secondary job for pocket money. Stay in college. Study, learn and ask questions. Be determined to be a doctor, a lawyer or an accountant. Learn a professional skill in which your unique skill will be compensated justly. Perhaps someday there will be enough Hispanics in our city who will stand up to the leeches who exploit our culture and say "enough . . . I will no longer listen to your bribery and flowery false adulation . . .

this music is ours and whatever fruits are derived from it are ours."
Then and only then will your chances in a musical career improve.

Symbolic Unity:
The Puerto Rican Day Parade

Introduction

• Today, the Puerto Rican Day Parade is recognized as the largest, most well-attended ethnic parade in New York City. Its sponsors affirm that it is "the largest outdoor cultural event in the whole United States." Indeed, beginning in 1959, it would always net a huge turn-out and the same uproarious enthusiasm and pride that it does today. (Jordan, 1994) However, it was barely mentioned in the press—at best it merited a photo in the centerfold of the popular press, the Daily News. At the time that the now deceased Dr. Rosa Estades was studying the history of the parade, it was not so recognized.

This article depicts the struggle of the first "pioneros" in this area to establish the parade. Subsequent struggles have consistently been waged. Included among these, the first attempts to have it covered by the Spanish-language television stations, then by the English-language press, finally, to have English-language television stations devote continuous coverage to it in 1991. The parade has come a long way in these regards, but it continues to be the same in many ways. It continues to demonstrate that every year, despite the obstacles, problems of the community, poverty, and politics, the show does go on—and it generally brings the house down.

Dr. Rosa Estades's work reflects the struggle of Puerto Rican scholars to write their own histories in their own words. Her work remains among the few to focus on what has been and continues to be a prominent institution in the community. It represents a major contribution to the history of Puerto Ricans and Latinos in the United States. Her chronicle of the parade's genesis allows us to understand the situation then, as well as the more contemporary situation. In the that

97

Puerto Ricans split from a more general Hispanic parade, so too more recent groups have and will develop their own parades as they increase in numbers. This does not necessarily imply a fractioning of the Latino population, rather a celebration of the differences within it. It is in the mutual and affirming commemoration of these differences that the inherent unity of Latinos is maintained.

In memory of Dr. Estades' contribution, a scholarship in her honor has been established at Hunter College with part of the proceeds of this volume. This article is similar to Max Salazár's article on Latin music in that both sought to accurately document important dimensions of the community that had been ignored and that are today major dimensions of the community.

SYMBOLIC UNITY:
THE PUERTO RICAN DAY PARADE

by Rosa Estades

' Ethnic traditions are kept alive in New York City in many different ways. Perhaps the most colorful of these ways is the use of parades. Most ethnic groups parade up Fifth Avenue at different times of the year displaying floats, bright banners, and representatives of the agencies and organizations serving the ethnic community.

' In the struggle to show unity and power Puerto Rican leaders organizing their parade (which they call *El Desfile*) continue to find themselves confronted with the issue of *hispanismo* versus *puertorriqueñismo*. There are those within the Puerto Rican community who criticize the parade and would like to have only one unified parade, i.e., one *Desfile Hispano*. They also express shock at the paraders and at the poor migrants who march; many would prefer to see a smaller parade exhibiting the most positive aspects of the heritage handed down by Spain to its colonies. For most Puerto Ricans, however, the *Desfile* represents a powerful show of strength and solidarity that far outweighs its negative aspects. For them this is one day when pride in their own identity overrides all other emotions. The sufferings and conflicts are forgotten—members of all factions join on this day and with a smile on their faces they march up Fifth Avenue, proud to be Puerto Rican.

The Desfile — Microcosm of the Community

Since their arrival, Puerto Rican migrants have identified with other Spanish-speaking groups. All the groups call themselves, and in

Dr. Rosa Estades was Associate Professor, Department of Educational Foundations, Hunter College, City University of New York, New York, N.Y.

turn are recognized by the overall New York City community, as *hispanos* or *latinos*. In setting themselves apart by stressing common ideals and patterns of behavior different from the dominant Anglo culture, Puerto Ricans find themselves sharing cultural similarities with those groups who speak Spanish and have a Hispanic tradition. A feeling of solidarity is developed, based on elements which are fundamental to the cultural nationalism of all the groups.

This solidarity was encountered by Mills, et al. (1950) in their study of the Harlem and Morrisania areas of New York City in 1948. They pointed to a possible growth of Spanish consciousness among Puerto Ricans in New York which could involve "the adoption of lifeways and social values somewhat different also from those of the generalized (middle class) American." They then pointed out the emergence of this consciousness in folkways and informal organizations (Mills, et al., 1950: 136). There is strong evidence to suggest that this feeling of *latino* identity rests first of all in a common language and in a community feeling maintained by the Spanish tradition in the New World. These aspects cut across particular nationalities and make these groups reject things American.

As Mills, et al. (1950) see it, this solidarity serves as a "core of resistance to assimilation . . . and the need for change of lifeways is thus placed within a larger pattern of conduct and feeling, which serves better than the Puerto Rican pattern to ease the shock, to avoid the conflict in American society . . . In their struggle to escape a minority position, they can thus reach and borrow prestige from some larger and more favored minority" (Mills, et al., 1950: 138).

This emerging consciousness continued to grow during the early fifties to the point that when Elena Padilla (1958) published her study of "Eastville," the word *hispanos* was cited as the preferred way Puerto Ricans refer to themselves in New York. Eastville was *El Barrio Latino*, or Spanish Harlem. This has continued to be so to a large extent; however, other factors have come into play in the situation, making the terms *puertorriqueños* and *puertorriqueñismo* also function as desired ways used by Puerto Ricans to refer to themselves.

The Hispanic Years

. The first parade was Hispanic; Puerto Ricans, by far the largest

100

Hispanic group, participated but they were not the organizers. There is a general consensus in the Puerto Rican and Hispanic communities of New York City that Jesús de Galíndez was the originator of the idea of all *hispanos* parading along Fifth Avenue to symbolize the unity and strength of their community. No one really knows how long Galíndez, a Spaniard and professor of languages at Columbia University, incubated the idea of the *Desfile*. His essays on East Harlem and his writing for the daily Spanish-language newspaper showed his keen interest in the community's future. Galíndez was aware of the socio-economic implications of the migration from Puerto Rico during the fifties and the future political importance of its growing numbers.

• The first organizing committee for the *Desfile Hispano* met in 1955 under Galíndez' leadership; its members represented a cross-section of Spaniards and Latin Americans, including representatives of the Puerto Rican community. This parade was to include flags from the different countries to emphasize the unity of all *hispanos*. Shortly before the first parade was to take place in 1956, Galíndez disappeared, a mystery which has not yet been solved. This was a blow to the organizers but the plans continued and on April 15, 1956, the first *Desfile Hispano* took place, with Antonio Méndez, the first Puerto Rican district leader from East Harlem, as the Grand Marshall. The *Segundo Desfile Pro Unidad Hispano* (Second Pro-Hispanic Unity Parade) was held in May, 1957, followed by another in 1958.

• There were conflicts from the very beginning among the organizers. The Puerto Rican group, growing in numbers, wanted to control the parade and thereby exert political pressure. In an internal confrontation, Puerto Ricans seceded for the purpose of organizing their own *Desfile*. In 1959, two parades were celebrated, the *Desfile Pro Unidad Hispano* and the first Puerto Rican parade. The following year a movement for unity was begun and a compromise reached whereby a Puerto Rican and a Hispanic parade were jointly celebrated. It was clear that Puerto Ricans would assume the leadership from then on. In 1961, however, two groups paraded. It was not until 1962 that the unification movement won and only one group paraded as the *Desfile Puertorriqueño*. The *Desfile* continued during the sixties as Puerto Rican until the Hispanic elements again decided to hold their own parade — the *Desfile de la Raza* — advocating the goal of Hispanic unity once more as their symbol. During the seventies two parades were held: the Puerto Rican in June and the Hispanic in

October, the latter honoring Columbus as the discoverer of America, which is in competition with the Italian parade, also in honor of Columbus.

The Puerto Rican Day Parade is Born

Among the factors that changed the original situation of self-identification as *hispanos* was the development of the Puerto Rican hometown groups. These groups, which were already very much in evidence during the 1920's, developed in large numbers during the fifties, to the point where they became one of the strongest influences on the organizational life of the community. These groups, which modeled themselves after pioneer clubs and organizations, grew rapidly in membership during the fifties. Belonging to these groups meant a reaffirmation not only of one's specific place of birth but generally of being a Puerto Rican. Another factor was the organization of the annual Puerto Rican parade. Even though Puerto Rican groups continued to participate in the *Desfile Hispano*, they eventually merged separately under the name of *El Desfile Puertor-riqueño*. Thus, the banners, floats, and symbolic unity of the community was mostly Puerto Rican in character and origin, while Hispanic elements were secondary. A third factor was the growth in population during the fifties and sixties, making the Puerto Rican community a potentially important political and economic entity in the life of the city. On self-examination, Puerto Ricans slowly found themselves belonging to a community which was increasingly representing itself not as *hispanos* but as *puertorriqueños*.

While this process of increasing solidarity and identification as *puertorriqueños* (as opposed to organizing under the more generic term of *hispanos*) was occurring, other factors were at work within the community to create factionalism. The most significant of these factors was the political status of the island and the consequent divisions of political parties in Puerto Rico.

The Impact of External Influences

In organizing for political representation, Puerto Ricans in the

United States face the divisions associated with the unsolved political status of the island. Puerto Ricans subscribe to different ideologies regarding the future political status of the island, whether statehood, independence or continuation of the present commonwealth status. In spite of the time spent in the United States, or even if born in the U.S., members of the community are divided on this issue. Since the political status is associated with and represented by different political parties in Puerto Rico, election results on the island are extremely important to Puerto Ricans in New York and in the United States and they strongly influence the nature of the Puerto Rican day parade.

During the first *Desfile* of 1959 and in the early sixties, the party favoring commonwealth status, the *Partido Popular Democrático*, was in power. It was a monolithic party with majority control in all branches of government. The mayors of the towns in Puerto Rico, dignitaries, and other representatives were the first to participate in the *Desfile*. The character and flavor of the parade, including its leadership, floats and banquets were greatly influenced by these first pro-commonwealth participants from Puerto Rico.

When the statehood party came into power in 1969 the *Desfile* was disrupted by elements favoring independence and radical changes for the island. In 1973, the *Partido Popular Democrático* returned to power and the *Desfile* went back to its former association with their leaders. More recently, during the 1976 election conventions, Ramón S. Vélez, former president of the *Desfile*, was snubbed by the pro-commonwealth ex-governor of Puerto Rico, Rafael Hernández Colón. Vélez subsequently backed the newly-elected New Progressive (pro-statehood) governor, Carlos Romero Barceló. Whatever happens in Puerto Rican electoral politics, the *Desfile* must confront the change of administration in Puerto Rico and the chances are that, as in the past, the parade will take center stage in this always conflictual situation.

The elements favoring independence for the island, who during the sixties disrupted the *Desfile*, march and chant slogans every year. To them the *Desfile* is a political farce that serves no purpose for the community. They use it to voice their own discontent and to ask for clemency for what they claim to be Puerto Rican political prisoners in jails in the United States and in Puerto Rico.

Another issue which complicates the organization of the parade

103

is the reaction of other groups in the city. The *Desfile*, with its approximately half a million participants and spectators, arouses deep feelings of hostility on the part of the overall New York community. These are expressed in complaints about the litter left behind after the parade and the noise and discomfort experienced by residents of middle and upper Fifth Avenue, who are exerting pressure to stop the *Desfile* and all other parades. The city administration has not complied with this request.

There are, however, others who identify with the parade, watch and enjoy it, perhaps reminiscing about the days when their own ethnic groups started their parades and thousands used to participate. The *Desfile* has, furthermore, stimulated other Puerto Rican communities outside New York City to organize their own parades. There are now parades in Chicago, New Jersey, upstate New York, Long Island, Connecticut, Boston, Philadelphia and Cleveland. These communities also invite mayors and dignitaries from Puerto Rico to honor them. So what New York began more than twenty years ago has become a nationwide trend among Puerto Rican communities.

The Organization of the Desfile Puertorriqueño

The backbone of the *Desfile* are the Puerto Rican hometown groups and mayors, and the New York State and City dignitaries, whether in the reviewing stand or as participants in the parade itself. It has developed over the years into a highly complex event which marks the highlight of community involvement. The *Desfile* is a predominantly grassroots movement; it is a day for *el pueblo* (the people) — even though most Puerto Ricans in all social classes participate or follow its progress.

Politicians, more than any other group, have profited from the *Desfile*. The mayor of New York, with an eye on the increasing number of Puerto Rican constituents, proclaims Puerto Rican week in June with good press coverage at City Hall. The annual banquet of the *Desfile* is increasingly a political event, where Puerto Rican and citywide politicians make appearances to please supporters.

The process of organization is complicated and difficult, involving all the divisions and factionalism which mirror the issues affecting the entire life of the community. The history of the organization of the

Desfile follows the ups and downs of the development of the community, reflecting the difficulties of the organizational life of Puerto Rican districts as they struggle for a place in the life of the city.

The leaders of the many groups and federations which participate are more interested in partisan politics than were the leaders of earlier civic and cultural pioneer organizations. They are more aware of their potential for power within the community and the large membership they represent. Through trips to Puerto Rico and through the organization of the *Desfile* they make valuable political contacts both in New York and in Puerto Rico. Although hampered in their political ambitions by lack of financial resources, leaders and organizations are turning to resources provided by the community–action programs of the anti-poverty agencies.

The elections for president and for other officers of the *Desfile* and the selection of a presiding Grand Marshall are usually accompanied by leadership struggles which involve the community for many months. This takes time and energy and the process has been criticized on the basis that these energies should be channelled in the direction of more profitable enterprises. To those who aspire to represent the migrants, however, the parade is tremendously important in terms of exposure, publicity and political opportunities.

Factions in control of important sectors of the organizations are usually involved in this contest for control. The hometown groups, through the *Congreso de Pueblos* (Congress of Hometown Groups) are caught in the middle of the conflict. Also, the newly-created organizations and agencies of the sixties have acquired a power base that can challenge other aspirants for representation. The control of the Puerto Rican Community Development Project and the Hunts Point Multi-Service Agency in the South Bronx, for example, gave Ramón S. Vélez a powerful base for controlling the Board of Directors of these agencies and also for controlling the committee for the *Desfile's* organization. For years Vélez was the undisputed leader of the *Desfile*. It still remains to be seen how his defeat in his 1976 bid for a Congressional seat will affect his leadership role in the community. Many forces are waging battles against Vélez' power base and the *Desfile* is also at the center of these struggles.

The administration of the funds for the parade creates another important issue. Fund-raising activities are constant throughout the year and money is a continuous problem. Accusations are often made against the controlling groups about the dispersal of funds. Groups have been hard put to explain money management to challenging groups and internal conflicts often arise on this issue.

Each parade has a history behind it. The growth and development of the *Desfile Puertorriqueño* reflects the growth and organization of the Puerto Rican community. In spite of the internal conflicts over funding, administration and factionalism, the leadership struggles and opposition in general, the *Desfile* is at the center of most of the issues which affect Puerto Ricans in New York. In this sense, the *Desfile* can be described as a microcosm of the community. New groups and organizations reflecting current ideologies and dedicating themselves to social/cultural affairs continue to emerge. The desire to preserve *puertorriqueñismo* continues to energize the parade. Furthermore, the increasing demand for spokespersons and representation for the Puerto Rican community at large strengthens the institutionalization of the *Desfile*.

REFERENCES

Mills, C. Wright, Clarence Senior and Rose K. Goldsen. The Puerto Rican Journey. New York: Harper and Row. 1950.

Padilla, Elena. Up From Puerto Rico. New York: Columbia University Press. 1958.

The Political Behavior
of New York Puerto Ricans:
Assimilation or Survival?

Introduction

At a time when most of the works in the literature paint-
ed a picture of the Puerto Rican community that was sharply
at odds with the realities as experienced by most Puerto
Ricans, Dr. Dale Nelson's article introduced an empirically-
based view that was more corresponding. The predominant
paradigm used in the English-language academic literature to
analyze Puerto Ricans (and other groups) was the assimilation paradigm (Rodríguez, 1995). This theory predicted the
sure demise, through assimilation, of the Puerto Rican community. Today, we see this did not happen. The Puerto Rican
community continues its vibrant traditions and its cultural
identity, although in continuous redefinition, has persevered
and resisted extinction.

Approaching the assimilation issue empirically and from
a political science perspective, Dr. Nelson found little support
for the Puerto Rican scenario drawn within this paradigm.
The theory predicted that in time immigrants assimilated,
and that this was reflected in their voting patterns. What he
found instead was that Puerto Ricans were assimilating but
that their voting patterns did not reflect significant differences from the first generation. The second generation did not
exhibit higher levels of political participation than the first
generation. Also, and contrary to the theory, Puerto Ricans
who married out did not engage in greater political participation; Puerto Ricans whose friends came from diverse ethnic
backgrounds did not participate more than those whose
friends were mainly Puerto Rican; the more assimilated
Puerto Ricans did not have attitudes that were more con-

ducive to participation, nor did their attitudes resemble those of assimilated members of other ethnic groups.

Moreover, the theory held that the style of Puerto Rican politics would be similar to that of other groups. Nelson found the style to be different, but not passive and dependent as at least one major work (i.e., Glazer & Moynihan, 1970) then argued. Although Puerto Ricans were less likely to vote, they were more active in protest demonstrations and more likely to join community organizations than other groups. Nelson provided an alternative explanation for low voting patterns in New York that more accurately reflected the times. This was that the New York experience was politically alienating for Puerto Ricans and that they had little desire to participate in a system that offered few rewards or incentives. Nelson's work was ahead of its time in that it presented a view that would subsequently come to be more closely examined. He argued that a distinctive subculture could be transmitted from one generation to another despite assimilation. This concept has come to be called "segmented assimilation" and it is increasingly used to explain the experiences of new immigrants to urban areas, such as Haitians and Latinos in Miami.

THE POLITICAL BEHAVIOR OF
NEW YORK PUERTO RICANS:
ASSIMILATION OR SURVIVAL?

by Dale C. Nelson

For decades the processes of assimilation and acculturation have been a major focus of research and analysis in ethnic studies. Until recently a broad consensus existed among social scientists on the nature, desirability, and inevitability of these related processes. Except for racial minorities, immigrant groups were expected to assimilate rapidly and to follow similar paths to complete submersion in the mainstream of American society. It has only been in the past 15 or 20 years that social scientists have come to question the inevitability of assimilation.

While sociologists have led the movement toward a critical re-evaluation of assimilation and its effects on immigrant groups, political scientists have lagged behind in considering the implications of the "new wisdom" for ethnic politics. Certainly the turbulent political events of the 1960's opened the eyes of many to the enduring nature of ethnic cleavages, but all too often the resurgence of ethnicity was viewed as a temporary aberration from "politics as usual." That events of the 1960's might have been signalling a more long-lasting ethnic basis for political division was a position taken by very few political analysts.

Even though the 1970's have witnessed a decline in the violent political outbreaks characteristic of the previous decade, ethnic politics continues to thrive. And social scientists have been slow to develop explanations for what is a puzzling phenomenon — namely, the persistence of strong ethnic attachments at the local level in the face of modernizing and socially integrative forces at the national

Dr. Dale C. Nelson is Associate Professor of Political Science, Fordham College at Rose Hill, Bronx, N.Y.

level. In the past few decades, some barriers to social integration have declined before the pressures of socioeconomic and geographic mobility. Also, a communications revolution increasingly provides people of diverse backgrounds with a common basis for evaluating and interpreting social and political events. And yet, in spite of all this, ethnic group life is thriving and ethnic political divisions are, if anything, becoming more acute.

The re-evaluation of the role of assimilation in ethnic life has focused on the slow rate at which it has occurred, especially in light of earlier predictions that the absorption of ethnic populations into the dominant Anglo society would be rapid. However, in the present paper I am less concerned with why assimilation has or has not followed its predicted course than with a more fundamental question: How useful are the dual concepts of assimilation and acculturation in explaining the political behavior of particular ethnic groups? I question whether one can speak of assimilation and acculturation as processes that uniformly apply to all ethnic populations and to all modes of socially-relevant behavior. In particular, it can be questioned whether assimilation and acculturation have so eroded Puerto Rican social structure and culture that a distinctive Puerto Rican political style no longer exists.

Is the more assimilated Puerto Rican more likely to participate in politics than the less assimilated Puerto Rican? Has acculturation diminished political-culture differences between Puerto Ricans and other ethnic groups—particularly those value orientations that act as stimuli to political participation? Do Puerto Ricans more frequently engage in particular *forms* of participation than other ethnic groups, or is the style of political participation roughly uniform across groups? These are the main questions this paper seeks to address.

There appears to be little agreement among scholars on how best to define the term "ethnicity." For purposes of this study, I will define it as the racial, religious, and/or nationality background characteristics of individuals. Data analysis is based on a survey conducted in the Washington Heights-Inwood section of Manhattan in 1973.[1] Six ethnic groups are represented among the 379 respondents, as follows: 50 Puerto Ricans, 78 Cubans, 61 Dominicans, 69 Jews, 58 Irish, and 63 blacks.[2]

Five forms of political participation will be examined. One form is *voting* in local (citywide) elections. The other four forms of participation are communal in nature. By *communal participation* I mean non-electoral participation where the individual acts in concert with other members of the community to solve community problems. The specific acts of communal participation to be examined are as follows: contacting public officials to deal with neighborhood problems, signing political petitions for neighborhood improvement, joining community problem-solving organizations, and attending neighborhood protest demonstrations.

Although assimilation and acculturation are related processes, they are conceptually distinct. *Assimilation* refers to the absorption of ethnic populations into the social system of the mainstream society. In terms of *primary* social relationships, this means a widening of friendship circles to include people of diverse ethnic backgrounds, and an increase in intergroup marriage rates. *Acculturation*, on the other hand, involves adoption of the dominant or mainstream culture. A vast body of literature describes the effects of both assimilation and acculturation on various ethnic groups. I shall refer to this literature as "assimilation theory."[3]

The most fundamental proposition that can be derived from assimilation theory is that assimilation and acculturation breed value and behavioral uniformity. In politics, this proposition translates into predictions about the level and style of political participation, and the nature of political value orientations (i.e., political culture). Assimilation is expected to bring about roughly similar levels of participation and comparable styles of political activity for all ethnic groups. Participation patterns are also expected to correspond to those of the white Anglo-Saxon Protestant majority. In addition, the acculturation process should create political value uniformities such that political beliefs and attitudes do not vary greatly along ethnic lines.

As a point of departure I will summarize a set of predictions or hypotheses derived from assimilation theory, and test these hypotheses with the survey data. In a later section I will explore some of the major implications of the findings for the political behavior of New York Puerto Ricans.

ASSIMILATION AND POLITICAL PARTICIPATION

The Role of Generation in the U.S.

Changes in the social, economic, and political behavior of immigrant populations have often been linked to differences between gen-

111

erations in the United States. First (or immigrant) generations often cling to the culture of the sending society, and tend to live and interact socially with their fellow ethnics. Many scholars maintain that second- and later-generation ethnics adopt the mainstream culture of the host society. As a result of social and economic mobility they tend to marry outside their ethnic group more than first-generation ethnics, and their friendship circles tend to be multi-ethnic. Second- and third-generation ethnics are expected to participate more in politics because they have come to identify with American society (not the "old country"), they no longer suffer from language barriers, and they have been socialized to participate in politics by the American school system. Thus, the first hypothesis centers on generational differences in political participation:

> *Hypothesis 1:* Second-generation Puerto Ricans will exhibit higher levels of political participation than first-generation Puerto Ricans.

Table 1. Participation in Political Activities, by Ethnicity and Generation in the United States (N=177)[a]

Percent Participating in Past Few Years by:	Puerto Ricans		Irish			Jews		
	1st	2nd	1st	2nd	3rd	1st	2nd	3rd
Contacting Public Officials	11	0	17	18	26	22	44	29
Signing Petitions	43	17	44	65	44	51	50	50
Joining Community Organizations	16	0	0	24	26	14	11	21
Attending Protest Demonstrations	11	0	0	13	9	8	22	0
Voting in Local Elections	55	33	88[b]	88	96	89[b]	83	79
(No. of Respondents)	(44)	(6)	(18)	(17)	(23)	(37)	(18)	(14)

Note: All data are rounded to the nearest whole percent in this and all tables to follow.

[a] Cubans and Dominicans were excluded from this table because there were no second-generation Cuban or Dominican respondents. Blacks were excluded because they are, by definition, at least third-generation Americans. More recent black West Indian and African immigrants were not included in the study.

[b] One Jewish and two Irish first-generation respondents were not U.S. citizens and were therefore ineligible to vote. These respondents were excluded from the calculations for voting.   112

Table 1 provides some rather interesting evidence on this hypothesis. The table shows that there is a dramatic *decline* between first- and second-generation Puerto Ricans in all five forms of political participation. The findings are especially impressive when compared to the effects of generation on Jewish and Irish respondents. In no case does participation decrease from first to second generation for the Irish, although for "contacting public officials" and "voting" there is no difference between first and second generations. For Jewish respondents the pattern is more mixed. Second-generation Jews are more likely to contact public officials and attend protest demonstrations than first-generation Jews, but there is essentially no difference between first- and second-generation Jews in signing petitions, joining community organizations, and voting. Thus, the hypothesis receives only partial support among Irish and Jewish respondents. Based on the small number of second-generation respondents (n=6), a note of caution is in order regarding the interpretation of generational differences among Puerto Ricans (and there were no third-generation Puerto Ricans in the study). But Hypothesis 1 clearly receives no support from the data.

Intermarriage and Multi-Ethnic Friendship Circles

The survey instrument has several questions which allow us to examine the effects of intermarriage and friendship circles on political participation.[4] Respondents were handed a list of ethnic groups and asked to identify the *one* group which best described most of their spouses' ancestors. Those who had married outside their ethnic group were placed in one category, and those who were married to a fellow ethnic were coded into a second category. Single people were excluded from the analysis. The resultant variable was labeled the "intermarriage rate."

For friendship circles, respondents were asked to identify their three best friends by first name only. The interviewer then handed respondents a list of ethnic groups and asked them to identify the ethnic background of each friend. A variable entitled "multi-ethnic friendships" was created by adding up the number of friends who did *not* share the respondent's ethnic background and dividing by three. In effect, the variable becomes the percentage of the three best friends who do not share the ethnic background of the respondent.

Using assimilation theory as a guide, we are now in a position to predict the effects of assimilation on the political behavior of Puerto Ricans. The first hypothesis addresses the effects of intermarriage, and the second predicts the impact of multi-ethnic friendship circles:

> *Hypothesis 2A:* Puerto Ricans who marry outside their ethnic group will participate in politics more often than Puerto Ricans who marry within their ethnic group.

Table 2A provides evidence for testing this hypothesis. For each of the five forms of political participation the table reports the percentage of respondents who have participated in the past few years, cross-tabulated by intermarriage rates.

Table 2A. Intermarriage and Political Participation Among Puerto Ricans (N=41)[a]

Percent Participating in Past Few Years by:	Married to Non-Puerto Rican	Married to Puerto Rican
Contacting Public Officials	9	7
Signing Petitions	46	33
Joining Community Organizations	9	17
Attending Protest Demonstrations	18	7
Voting in Local Elections	55	53
(No. of Respondents)	(11)	(30)

[a]Nine respondents were single (never married) and were therefore excluded from the table.

The data reported in Table 2A present a mixed picture in relation to the prediction stated in Hypothesis 2A. In terms of signing petitions and attending protest demonstrations, the more assimilated Puerto Ricans are more likely to participate than the less assimilated Puerto Ricans. However, for both of these forms of participation, differences between the assimilated and non-assimilated are not large (i.e., 13 and 11 percent). For contacting public officials and voting, there is essentially no difference between the more and the less assimilated Puerto Ricans. Finally, the *less* assimilated are slightly more likely to join community problem-solving organizations than the more assimilated (i.e., 17 percent to 9 percent, respectively). When the relationship between intermarriage and political participation was examined among the other five ethnic groups in the study, the results were similar to those obtained for Puerto Ricans. Thus, although the data provide some support for the hypothesis, intermarriage generally does not have the effects that were predicted.

It can be argued that intermarriage need not be a chief source of increased participation among ethnic groups for the assimilation thesis to be valid. Instead, it may be that the nature of friendship circles affects political participation more. Specifically, assimilation theory suggests that participation levels will be higher among those who are involved in multi-ethnic friendship circles than they are for ethnics who tend to choose friends among their own group. Recent studies point to the importance of friendship circles as agents of political socialization. Some authors have even argued that friendship circles are replacing family networks as the primary source of political socialization among children and adults (see, e.g., Dawson and Prewitt, 1969). If friendship networks provide strong cues for political involvement, assimilation theory suggests that the more diverse the friendship circle the more likely the individual is to receive encouragement for political participation.

Hypothesis 2B: Puerto Ricans whose friends come from diverse ethnic backgrounds will participate more in politics than Puerto Ricans whose friends are mostly Puerto Rican.

In order to test this hypothesis, I classified all respondents in the study into two groups: those with diverse friendships and those with mostly ethnic friends. I constructed a variable, "percent of three best friends who are ethnic," and used the median of the entire sample (n=379) to divide respondents into one or the other group. Table 2B reports the percent of Puerto Rican participants for each of the five forms of participation, cross-tabulated by the nature of friendship circles.

The data in Table 2B do not support Hypothesis 2B. The nature of Puerto Rican friendship patterns has no effect on the contacting of public officials. Puerto Ricans who are part of multi-ethnic friendship groups are only slightly more likely to sign petitions, join community organizations, and attend protest demonstrations than the less assimilated Puerto Ricans. It is only for *voting* that the hypothesis finds support: the more assimilated Puerto Ricans are about 24 percent more likely to vote than the less assimilated Puerto Ricans. The more

Table 2B. Multi-Ethnic Friendship Circles and Puerto Rican Political Participation (N=50)

Percent Participating in Past Few Years by:	Diverse Ethnic Friendships	Mostly Puerto Rican Friends
Contacting Public Officials	10	11
Signing Petitions	42	37
Joining Community Organizations	16	11
Attending Protest Demonstrations	13	5
Voting in Local Elections	61	37
(No. of Respondents)	(31)	(19)

assimilated black, Cuban, and Dominican respondents were also more likely to vote; paradoxically, it was the *less* assimilated Irish and Jewish respondents who exhibited the highest voting levels. However, for the other five ethnic groups, the nature of one's friendship circles had virtually no effect on *communal* participation items (i.e., for all forms of participation except voting). Based on the findings for Puerto Ricans and the other ethnic groups in the study, we must reject Hypothesis 2B.

Up to this point our analysis has provided little support for two fundamental predictions about political behavior derived from assimilation theory — namely, that intermarriage and multi-ethnic friendship circles are associated with higher levels of political participation among Puerto Ricans. In the next section we will examine another important dimension of assimilation theory, i.e., the role of acculturation in Puerto Rican political behavior.

ACCULTURATION AND POLITICAL BEHAVIOR

According to assimilation theory, acculturation is the natural byproduct of assimilation. That is, as immigrant groups become assimilated to American society, they are expected to adopt the culture of the dominant or mainstream society, including its political culture. By *political culture* I mean the values, beliefs, and norms that guide individual and group political activity. Triandis (1972), among others, maintains that cultural values are best measured by clusters of attitudes. Thus, political culture can be measured by political attitudes

116

which set apart different social groups.

In this section we will explore three aspects of assimilation theory as it relates to political acculturation among Puerto Ricans and other ethnic groups: (1) the relationship between assimilation and political attitudes, (2) the effects of socioeconomic status on political attitudes, and (3) ethnic styles of political participation.

Political Attitudes and Assimilation

If assimilation theory is valid, the more assimilated Puerto Ricans should exhibit political attitudes and beliefs that are different from the less assimilated Puerto Ricans. In fact, the more assimilated members of all immigrant ethnic groups should have roughly similar political attitudes and beliefs.

Many research studies have demonstrated that holding certain beliefs and attitudes toward politics is highly correlated with political participation (see, e.g., Verba and Nie, 1972). Specifically, those who express a strong interest in politics, follow political news, and are knowledgeable about politics tend to participate more than people who express little political interest or awareness. Likewise, people who feel politically efficacious (i.e., believe that they personally can have an effect by taking political action) are also most likely to actually participate in politics. At the local level, people who are aware of community problems and the actions of local groups and organizations to deal with these problems are also more likely to participate in community-level politics. Lastly, the degree to which people trust local officials to act in the community's best interest also affects whether or not people become politically active.[5]

Taken together these attitudes form the core of what may be termed *participant political culture.*[6] People who express these beliefs and attitudes are much more likely to participate in politics than people who do not. Assimilation theory suggests that assimilation leads to higher levels of participant culture. Writers from Tocqueville (1948) to Almond and Verba (1965) have claimed that mainstream Americans are highly active in political affairs, especially when one compares the United States with other nations of the world. It follows that if assimilation leads to acculturation, immigrant groups will adopt a more participant political culture. Thus, as Puerto Ricans become more assimilated, assimilation theory suggests that they will exhibit more participant-oriented political attitudes and beliefs.

> *Hypothesis 3:* The more assimilated Puerto Ricans will exhibit political attitudes more conducive to participation than the less assimilated Puerto Ricans; in addition, their political attitudes will be similar to the more assimilated members of other ethnic groups.

In order to test this hypothesis, an index of participant political culture was constructed and dichotomized into attitudes more and less supportive of political participation. Because there were vast differences between ethnic groups in the degree to which their members exhibited attitudes supportive of participation, the participant-culture index was divided at the median for *each* ethnic group. The intermarriage and multi-ethnic friendship variables examined earlier were also combined to form an index of assimilation. The participant-culture index was then cross-tabulated with the assimilation index for each ethnic group in the survey sample. Table 3 reports the results.

The findings in Table 3 strongly refute the first part of the hypothesis, i.e., that assimilated Puerto Ricans exhibit political attitudes more conducive to political participation. Whereas about 46 percent of highly assimilated Puerto Ricans express a strong participant culture, a full 62 percent of the less assimilated Puerto Ricans are participant-oriented. The Puerto Rican pattern contrasts sharply with all other ethnic groups in the study. For Jewish respondents the more and the less assimilated exhibit roughly the *same* level of participant political culture (i.e., 48 and 46 percent). The fact that the assimilated Puerto Ricans diverge so greatly from the more assimilated of other ethnic groups is, on the surface, somewhat perplexing. Why should the more assimilated Puerto Ricans be less politically-oriented?

In order to further explore this anomaly, the participant political-culture index was cross-tabulated by generation in the United States. As was noted earlier, second-generation Puerto Ricans appear to be less participatory than first-generation Puerto Ricans. It is conceivable that low participation is a function of the weak development of participant-oriented political attitudes among the second generation. The data, however, reveal *no difference* between first and second generation in levels of participant political culture.

The second part of Hypothesis 3, also based on assimilation

Table 3. Percent Exhibiting Strong and Weak Participant Political Culture, by Assimilation Level and Ethnicity (N=317)[a]

Assimilation Level

Participant Culture	Puerto Ricans		Jews		Irish		Blacks		Dominicans		Cubans	
	High	Low	High	Low	High	Low	High	Low	High	Low	High	Low
Strong	46	62	48	46	61	42	50	43	60	36	53	41
Weak	54	38	52	54	39	58	50	57	40	64	47	59
Total Percent	100	100	100	100	100	100	100	100	100	100	100	100
(No. of Respondents)	(28)	(13)	(21)	(35)	(18)	(24)	(20)	(30)	(30)	(25)	(36)	(37)

[a]Sixty-two respondents were single and were therefore excluded from the table.

theory, maintains that the more assimilated members of all ethnic groups will have roughly similar political attitudes. That is, the homogenizing effects of assimilation will erase ethnic group attitudinal differences. Table 3A provides evidence to test this thesis. Only respondents who scored above the *sample* median on the assimilation index were included. The table reports the percent of (assimilated) respondents in each ethnic group who scored above the sample median on the participant-culture index.

Table 3A. Percent of Assimilated Respondents Above the Sample Median on the Participant Political-Culture Index, by Ethnic Group (N=153)

Ethnic Group	(No.)	Participant Political-Culture Index
Irish	(18)	89
Blacks	(20)	80
Jews	(21)	76
Puerto Ricans	(28)	43
Cubans	(36)	28
Dominicans	(30)	17

Again it is necessary to reject the stated hypothesis. Controlling for level of assimilation, there are vast differences in political attitudes among ethnic groups. At one end of the scale, a full 89 percent of the assimilated Irish respondents exhibit participant-oriented attitudes, whereas only 17 percent of the assimilated Dominicans do. Assimilation apparently does not lead to a homogenized political culture among ethnic groups. And Puerto Rican political attitudes are *strikingly* different from those of the other ethnic groups in the study.

If our earlier findings provided any support for assimilation theory, the data on the relationship between political attitudes and assimilation raise some serious doubts about its validity. Assimilated Puerto Ricans are less rather than more likely to exhibit political attitudes supportive of political participation. Second-generation Puerto Ricans are neither more nor less likely to exhibit a strong participant political culture than first-generation Puerto Ricans. Finally, the more assimilated members of all ethnic groups in the study vary greatly in their levels of participant culture. Thus, Hypothesis 3 cannot be supported by the data.

The Role of Socioeconomic Status (SES)

A strong consensus exists among social scientists on the role of socioeconomic status in political participation. Many studies ·have demonstrated that individuals with higher incomes, better education, and more prestigious occupations (e.g., professionals) tend to be more politically active than low-status individuals.

Studies of political participation have further uncovered a strong association between socioeconomic status and participant political culture. High status individuals are noted for their strong interest in politics, high sense of political efficacy, strong community awareness, and critical orientation to government officials and agencies (Verba and Nie, 1972; Milbrath and Goel, 1977). Because the present study includes ethnic groups varying widely in their levels of socioeconomic status, one possible explanation for participant-culture differences among the ethnic groups is that they are the result of social-class differences. Thus, if socioeconomic status is held constant, that is, if one compares the political attitudes of middle-class respondents in all ethnic groups, there should be no major ethnic differences. Similarly, if the political attitudes of working-class respondents are compared, they should not vary along ethnic lines.

Hypothesis 4: Once socioeconomic status is held constant, Puerto Rican political attitudes will not differ significantly from those of other ethnic groups.

To test the thesis that socioeconomic status differences between Puerto Ricans and other ethnic groups account for the distinctiveness of Puerto Rican political attitudes, the dichotomized participant-culture index was cross-tabulated for all ethnic groups, controlling for socioeconomic status. The SES variable, an additive index which combines yearly income, educational level and occupational prestige, was dichotomized into "high status" and "low status" for ease of presentation. The dividing line between low and high status is the sample average or mean. Table 4 reports the results.

The data in Table 4 provide evidence for a strong rejection of the

Table 4. Percent of Respondents With Above-Average Participant Political Culture by Ethnic Group, Controlling for Socioeconomic Status (N=379)

Ethnic Group	(No.)	Low SES	(No.)	High SES	(No.)
Puerto Ricans	(50)	37	(27)	48	(23)
Jews	(69)	58	(12)	70	(57)
Irish	(58)	50	(16)	95	(42)
Blacks	(63)	71	(35)	79	(28)
Cubans	(78)	14	(52)	42	(26)
Dominicans	(61)	8	(48)	39	(13)

SES thesis. Among low-status ethnics, there is a remarkable 63 percent range between ethnic groups exhibiting the highest and lowest participant-culture levels (i.e., blacks and Dominicans). Puerto Rican participant culture is about midway between the highest and lowest levels, but clearly *different* from all other ethnic groups.

Among high-status (or middle-class) respondents, ethnic group differences are also large. About 95 percent of the Irish middle-class respondents exhibit strong participant cultures, compared to only 39 percent of the Dominican middle-class respondents. Puerto Rican political attitudes are not much different from Dominican or Cuban attitudes, but all three Hispanic groups exhibit weaker participant cultures than black and white ethnic groups. Thus, although middle-class ethnic differences are smaller than those among low-status (working-class) ethnics, they are nevertheless substantial.

The thesis, then, that differences in ethnic political attitudes are merely the result of socioeconomic status differences between ethnic groups finds very little support in the data. Rather, the findings suggest that ethnic political cultures are resistant to modification brought about by socioeconomic mobility, at least for some ethnic groups. Socioeconomic mobility has little effect on the political attitudes of Puerto Ricans. There is only an 11 percent difference in participant culture between high- and low-status Puerto Ricans (i.e., 37 vs. 48 percent). For blacks and Jews high- and low-status differences are also small (i.e., about 12 and 8 percent, respectively). However, socioeconomic status does appear to have an important impact on the political attitudes of Cubans, Dominicans and, in particular, the Irish.

In the 1950's Robert E. Lane (1959) argued that ethnic groups exhibited distinctive styles of political participation which reflected differences in ethnic subcultural values. By style I mean the tendency for individuals or groups to select certain modes of participation (e.g., voting) over other modes. Lane, for example, notes that the Irish are particularly active voters. He also identifies Jews as particularly likely to write letters to government officials. He explains these patterns or styles of participation by maintaining that "ethnic subcultures place their stamp upon the 'appropriate' areas of participation for the individual" (Lane, 1959: 68).

Many authors disagree with the thesis that ethnic subcultures continue to guide political behavior. Parenti (1967), for example, claims that acculturation to American values is so rapid that ethnic subcultures are no longer relevant to ethnic political participation. And Parenti's position is more consistent with the dominant views of assimilation theorists than Lane's. Thus, assimilation theory suggests that patterns (or styles) of Puerto Rican political participation will not be different from the participation styles of other ethnic groups.

> *Hypothesis 5:* The style of Puerto Rican political participation will *not* be significantly different from that of other ethnic groups.

To test the thesis that the acculturation process has eliminated or sharply reduced political-style differences between Puerto Ricans and other groups, each of the five forms of participation examined earlier was cross-tabulated with ethnicity. Only respondents who had participated in at least one of the five forms were included in the table. Since the concern here is not the fact that ethnic groups participate at different rates, the amount of ethnic group participation was held constant. Table 5, then, reports the degree to which *participants* in all ethnic groups of the study select the same or different forms of participation.

The data in Table 5 reveal some interesting political-style differences between Puerto Ricans and other ethnic groups. About 22 percent of Puerto Rican participants have contacted a public official; this is considerably different from Dominican (11 percent) and, par-

Table 5. Percent of Participants Engaging in Each Form of Political Participation, by Ethnic Group (N=173)

Participation	Puerto Ricans	Jews	Irish	Blacks	Dominicans	Cubans
Contacting Officials	22	49	38	42	11	13
Joining Organizations	30	24	31	39	39	9
Signing Petitions	87	85	91	86	78	91
Attending Protests	22	17	16	22	11	9
Voting in Local Elections	70	88[a]	90[a]	78	—[a]	79[a]
(No. of Respondents)	(23)	(41)	(32)	(36)	(18)	(23)

[a] Because some respondents were not United States citizens, the percentages reported for voting are based on a different number of cases: Jews, 40; Irish, 30; Cubans, 14; Dominicans, 4. For the latter group, there were too few cases to analyze.

ticularly, Jewish participants (49 percent). Puerto Rican and black participants are the most active in protest demonstrations (22 percent), compared to Cubans (9 percent), who are the least active. Puerto Ricans (30 percent) are considerably more likely than Cubans (9 percent) and, to a lesser extent, Jews (24 percent) to join community organizations, but less likely than both Dominican and black activists (39 percent). Puerto Rican activists are the least likely of all groups to vote (70 percent), and there is about a 20 percent difference between Puerto Rican and Irish activists. It is only in signing petitions that ethnic group activists are about equal in their participation rates.

Thus, the data do not support the thesis that political-style differences no longer exist between Puerto Ricans and other ethnic groups. Puerto Rican participants are very active in protesting and signing petitions, active in community organizations, moderately active in contacting public officials, and weak in voting participation, relative to political activists in other ethnic groups. Based on the data in Table 5, it is necessary to reject the argument that ethnic subcultural values no longer affect the style of Puerto Rican political participation.

CONCLUSION

Having failed to confirm any of the hypotheses based on assimilation theory, the implications of the findings are in need of discussion. Because the size of the Puerto Rican sample is small, several of the findings based on *internal* differences between Puerto Ricans (e.g., between first- and second-generation respondents) must be viewed as suggestive rather than definitive. However, the inability of assimilation theory to satisfactorily explain the aspects of Puerto Rican political behavior we examined raises some serious questions about the theory itself. If assimilation theory is faulty, it is desirable to suggest some alternative explanations.

With regard to participation differences between first- and second-generation Puerto Ricans, assimilation theory does not account for a situation in which the American experience of an immigrant group acts to *suppress* participation. It is conceivable that the socialization experience of Puerto Ricans in Puerto Rico is more supportive of participation than that of New York Puerto Ricans. Since the 1940's, voting turnout, for example, has often been higher in Puerto Rico than on the United States mainland. Assimilation theory implies that *all* immigrant groups arrive in this country with a political culture less supportive of participation than American political culture. Such a theory does not account for the possibility that socialization to American culture could decrease the propensity of some immigrant groups to participate in politics.

The low level of political involvement exhibited by second-generation Puerto Ricans does not fit well with assimilation theory. By such objective measures as intermarriage and multi-ethnic friendship patterns, the second generation is *more* assimilated than the first generation, so failure to assimilate cannot account for lower participation rates in the second generation. The data are perhaps more consistent with the thesis that the New York experience is *politically alienating* for Puerto Ricans. Few Puerto Ricans have been elected to public office and, with the exception of Herman Badillo, none has developed a citywide or national presence. It may be that second-generation Puerto Ricans have little desire to participate actively in a political system that offers them few tangible rewards or incentives. In a period when government at all levels appears to be retrenching from its earlier commitment to social and economic programs for the ethnic poor, the decline in Puerto Rican political involvement may even accelerate.

With the exception of the effects of multi-ethnic friendships on voting, assimilation variables did not fare well as explanations of Puerto Rican political participation. The absence of association between levels of assimilation and political acculturation was particularly striking. Occupying a middle position between the stronger participant orientation of blacks and white ethnics, and the weaker participant orientations of Cubans and Dominicans, Puerto Rican political attitudes were clearly distinct. Furthermore, holding socioeconomic status constant did not eliminate the strong attitudinal differences between Puerto Ricans and other ethnic groups analyzed. As Laumann (1973), Lenski (1961), Greeley (1974) and others maintain, *cultural pluralism* appears to be very much alive.

That distinctive political subcultures can be transmitted from one generation to another *despite* assimilation suggests that cultural differences among ethnic groups are unlikely to dissipate at the rapid rate indicated by assimilation theory. Thus, cultural values distinctive to Puerto Ricans are likely to affect their levels of participation into the foreseeable future. The rather strong style differences between Puerto Rican participants and activists in other ethnic groups add even further support to the contention that cultural diversity is likely to loom large as an explanatory factor in ethnic political behavior.

The concepts of assimilation and acculturation are of little explanatory power in examining patterns of Puerto Rican political behavior. The more assimilated Puerto Rican is not much different from the less assimilated Puerto Rican when it comes to levels of participation, styles of participation, or levels or participant culture. Under these circumstances, research may be more fruitfully focused on the ways that culture influences patterns of political behavior, than on assimilation and acculturation per se.

NOTES

1. The survey was part of the New York City Neighborhood Project, Bureau of Applied Social Research (BASR), Columbia University. The project was funded by the RANN Division of the National Science Foundation (NSF). I wish to thank the directors of BASR and NSF for their support. Parts of this article appeared previously in the Research Bulletin, Vol. 1, No. 4, October 1978. I am grateful to Dr. Lloyd Rogler, Director of the Hispanic Research Center, Fordham University, and Editor of the Research Bulletin, for his permission to reproduce parts of that earlier article.

2. The size of the overall survey sample and the roughly equal number of respondents in each ethnic group provide for *inter*-group comparisons that generally do not raise questions about the statistical significance of our findings. However, when *intra*-group analysis is involved, the small size of each ethnic group limits our ability to establish the statistical significance of the findings. For this reason, findings involving intra-group comparisons among Puerto Ricans should be viewed as *suggestive* rather than *definitive*.

3. For an excellent survey and critical review of assimilation theory, see Gordon (1964) and Greeley (1974).

4. In his now classic work on the topic of assimilation, Gordon (1964) has demonstrated how difficult the term "assimilation" is to conceptualize. He describes several forms of assimilation and points out that the assimilation process occurs at both the *primary* (i.e., family, friends, workplace) and *secondary* (i.e., residential, organizational, and institutional) levels of social relationships. If assimilation is difficult to grasp conceptually, it is equally difficult to develop adequate empirical indicators which fully measure it. I have selected friendship and intermarriage patterns to represent assimilation in the analysis because they are the most common threads running through the various definitions of assimilation in the literature. However, they are only *partial* measures of assimilation; thus, a note of caution is in order in interpreting the data that follow.

5. Actually, there is considerable controversy over the role of political trust in political participation. See my article (Nelson, 1979) for a more extensive discussion of the five attitudes considered. In my own data I found a strong positive correlation between political *distrust* (cynicism) and political participation.

6. Almond and Verba (1965) coined the term "participant political culture" to apply to nations. There is no reason, however, why the term cannot be applied to subnational groups.

REFERENCES

Almond, Gabriel A. and Sidney Verba. The Civic Culture. Boston: Little, Brown & Co. 1965.

Dawson, Richard E. and Kenneth Prewitt. Political Socialization. Boston: Little, Brown & Co. 1969.

Gordon, Milton M. Assimilation in American Life. New York: Oxford University Press. 1964.

Greeley, Andrew M. Ethnicity in the United States. New York: John Wiley & Sons. 1974.

Lane, Robert E. Political Life. New York: Free Press. 1959.

Laumann, Edward O. Bonds of Pluralism. New York: John Wiley & Sons. 1973.

Lenski, Gerhard. The Religious Factor. Garden City, N.Y.: Doubleday & Co. 1961.

Milbrath, Lester W. and M. L. Goel. Political Participation. 2nd ed. Chicago: Rand McNally. 1977.

Nelson, Dale C. "Ethnicity and socioeconomic status as sources of participation: The case for ethnic political culture." American Political Science Review 73 (December). 1979.

Parenti, Michael. "Ethnic politics and the persistence of ethnic identification." American Political Science Review 61 (September). 1967.

Tocqueville, Alexis de. Democracy in America. New York: ed. Phillips Bradley. 1948.

Triandis, Harry C. The Analysis of Subjective Culture. New York: John Wiley & Sons. 1972.

Verba, Sidney and Norman H. Nie. Participation in America. New York: Harper & Row. 1972.

The Struggle
for Local Community Control

Introduction

The author of this article was the first Puerto Rican educator to serve as a district superintendent in New York City schools. Two Bridges, or Community District 1, in Manhattan's Lower East Side educated a diverse population: 73% were Puerto Rican, 8% were Chinese or of Chinese ancestry, 15% were African American and the remainder was composed of white ethnics. It was one of three contested educational arenas (the others were Ocean-Hill Brownsville and I.S. 201 in Harlem) that figured in the militant struggles of the community control and decentralization movements of the late 1960s and early 1970s.

The mobilization for community control emerged in response to a school integration model that posited removing youngsters from neighborhood schools to predominantly white, supposedly superior institutions. Although Puerto Rican children comprised the overwhelming majority of the district's children, Puerto Rican parents were essentially removed from the decision-making process. They joined with other Community District 1 activists and engaged in "one of the longest and most bitterly fought campaigns for the rights of Puerto Rican and other community students and parents" (Nieto, 1994). Along with African-American activists, they had long supported two-way integration models and believed that improving the quality of education, rather than busing children to unfamiliar, potentially explosive surroundings, was in the best interests of all involved. Through the electoral process, they gained majority control of the Community District 1 school board. They enacted changes such as bilingual instruction, a systematized reading program and the hiring of Dr. Fuentes as superintendent. Charging that the schools had become "arenas of political extremism, racism and patronage," the United Federation of Teachers joined forces with the Board of Education and the Council of Supervisory Associations to regain control of the schools. In 1974, the school board was restored to a white majority and Dr. Fuentes was dismissed.

Fuentes' account is perhaps the first to chronicle the events of a community's struggle for control of neighborhood schools from an "insider" perspective. He was an educator who understood the pedagogical needs of Puerto Rican and other minority students. His article in this volume focuses on the formation of an alliance between two powerful and historically oppositional unions, the United Federation of Teachers and the Council of Supervisory Associations, against the child-centered interests of the community. It reflects the outrage of one who executed a pivotal role in a skewed, uneven challenge, and underscores the grass-roots nature of the resistance.

At a time when bilingual programs for Puerto Rican and other Spanish dominant youngsters were in their infancy, when the licensure of bilingual teachers had just commenced (1967), and before the ASPIRA Consent Decree (1974) mandated instruction in languages other than English, the struggles of Community District 1 served as a beacon for Puerto Rican self-determination, definition and solidarity. Today Fuentes, a professor in the School of Education of the University of Massachusetts, Amherst, argues that many of the educational opportunities available to New York City students had their genesis in the community struggles of the sixties and early seventies.

THE STRUGGLE FOR
LOCAL POLITICAL CONTROL
by Luis Fuentes

Throughout the mid-sixties the leadership of the United Federation of Teachers (UFT), including its President, Albert Shanker, was mildly progressive. It marched with the Rev. Martin Luther King and gave the impression of supporting the integration movement in New York City. As late as 1967, its contract and strike issues were directed at changing the slum schools. Admittedly, its reform effort — the More Effective Schools program — was ill-advised, costly and ineffectual. Nonetheless, the 1967 contract represented the union's final effort at even appearing to care. Throughout this period Shanker was a vulnerable president, without a personal constituency within the union, and with a serious potential leadership challenge from the left. He had little citywide labor influence and even less political influence.

I want to concentrate my attention on an analysis of two unions — the United Federation of Teachers (UFT) and the Council of Supervisory Associations (CSA). I don't want my discussion of these forces to be distorted. I am not anti-union. But I firmly believe that the current leadership of these unions bears no relationship to the historic and decent impulse of working people to organize. I ask you to consider this fact: the CSA is an association of supervisors, namely the principals and bureaucrats who have historically been the core of this educational system. It is in fact a union for management. The UFT and its national organization, the American Federation of Teachers (AFT), as labor unions for teachers, were born in part out of widespread dissatisfaction with the National Education Association

Dr. Luis Fuentes is Professor Emeritus of the School of Education, University of Massachusetts, Amherst, Massachusetts.

(NEA), which remains the largest teacher organization in America. The basic criticism of the NEA offered by the David Seldens and Albert Shankers who built the AFT was that the old NEA was dominated by supervisors. Throughout the early history of the UFT, the union saw the supervisors and the supervisors' organization, the CSA, as a major opponent. This opposition was suddenly transformed into a firm alliance in 1967-68 when supervisors and teachers' organizations perceived a common foe — black and Puerto Rican parents and community. Not once, since 1968, have these organizations opposed each other. A supposedly workers' union is thus in complete alliance with a management association.

Union Gains from Teacher Strikes

The 1968 teacher strikes in New York City were the system's reaction to the rising tide of the black and brown liberation movements. Somehow the UFT union's confrontation with the people of Ocean Hill in Brooklyn became the system's solitary answer to an entire network of related national pressures. These strikes would settle the city's fate until a new generation raised the issues in another form. Inside the events of 1967 and 1968, inside the schools of Ocean Hill and Intermediate School 201 in Harlem the union made its war on the children of the poor.

The union substituted its power for the power of a Board of Education which had been partly re-shaped by the rising force of black and brown liberation. It identified the bulwarks of the system — the Council of Supervisory Associations, the Board of Examiners, the professional bureaucracy — and aligned itself with these forces, transforming them into its own dependent stepchildren. The UFT went to the state capitol in Albany and whiplashed legislators into writing its will into law. Ocean Hill was broken, Intermediate School 201 in Harlem was broken, and an administrative shuffling of the cards called "decentralization legislation" was adopted.[1] The effort to liberate black and brown schools was broken and so was the tide that promised to alter our history.

The events of 1968 transformed the union and its leadership. The UFT wholly abandoned its progressive pretensions. The reward (in 1969) was the most lucrative contract in the history of public-employee collective bargaining. The salary, pension and welfare gains were so extraordinary that the contract has been widely regarded not as the result of a negotiation but of a capitulation.

In the nine years that followed this contract, the school system lost 18,000 teaching positions while the average teacher salary almost doubled. A confidential internal survey contracted by Shanker and taken by Daniel Yankelovich, the professional polling agency, estimated that in 1972, before later contract gains, the average family income of a UFT teacher-member was $28,000. The 1972 contract concentrated its increments at the top of the salary scale, gaining only $300 for new teachers by 1975 but $4,000 for those at the maximum-salary step. These increases made it possible for a new teacher in 1968 to triple his income by 1975 and to retire at a typical rate of 75 percent of his final year's pay. More than anywhere else in America, the New York City teacher had made it. In crushing community control in I.S. 201 and Ocean Hill, the union had saved the system. Now it contractually owned it.

But the union obscured what it had done in Ocean Hill by using the smokescreen devices of due process and anti-Semitism (N.Y.C. Civil Liberties Union, 1970). The success of these weapons in 1968 made them the cornerstone of union power. The mass media completed the equation for Shanker: black and brown community control equals mob control; blacks and browns are incapable of granting due process to whites and are inflamed with a virulent brand of anti-Semitism. These have been the UFT's weapons wherever people still talk about controlling their own schools.

The Production of Illiterates and Junkies

There is one issue perhaps that demonstrates best the total opposition of these unions to any positive change: bilingual education. I was a superintendent selected by a community whose school district consisted of youngsters who were 73 percent Puerto Rican, 15 percent black, and eight percent Chinese, with the remainder being Jewish, Polish, Ukrainian, Indian, and Italian. Eighty-five percent of these youngsters by the time they reach the eighth grade are functional illiterates — three to four years behind grade level in reading. There are those who call these statistics a sign of failure; but if 85 percent of the products of any industry shared a basic characteristic, we would assume that it was the intention of the industry to mark its products with that characteristic. The 15 percent of the products not so marked with this characteristic would be the ones considered abnormal. So I must conclude that the 15 percent of the children in my district who graduate from our schools able to read at their grade level are abnormal. The system is 85 percent *successful*. Illiteracy is its product (Fuentes, 1973).

There is no great mystery to these statistics. There are 2,000 children in District 1 who speak no English at all, and 4,000 who speak it so hesitantly that they cannot be understood. When I came to District 1, there were over 800 regular teachers in the twenty schools of our district. Six spoke Spanish. One, Chinese. Our teachers and students could not even talk to each other.

District 1, in the Lower East Side of Manhattan, is illustrative of a broader series of facts. Let's look at some numbers to learn something about Puerto Rican youngsters in the city of New York. Startling figures for the early 1970's indicate that close to 45 percent of the city's Puerto Rican males aged 18 to 25 are unemployed, the highest for any racial/ethnic group in the city. (Keep in mind that the unemployment figures apply only to those actively *seeking* work and that many young Puerto Ricans by their early twenties have already stopped trying.) Fifty-three percent of the city's Puerto Rican student population drop out of school; 26 percent of the state's narcotics addicts under treatment are Puerto Rican and 82 percent of the Puerto Rican addicts are school dropouts. That is why Puerto Rican parents have come to view their schools as junkie production lines, since statistically they produce almost twice as many junkies as literates. The 1970 New York City school census identified 117,469 Spanish-dominant, non-English-speaking pupils. Despite the fact that 25 percent of the city's student population is Puerto Rican, less than five percent of its professional staff is Puerto Rican. There is roughly one Puerto Rican teacher for every 300 Puerto Rican students in New York schools, isolating Puerto Rican children from their own culture, background and language.

The Manipulation of Racial Fears

District 1's schools are 96 percent minority in pupil enrollment, including 73 percent Puerto Rican. Yet the total adult population of the school district — note, I said the *total adult population* — is over 50 percent white. This does not mean that the white adults are having black, Puerto Rican, and Chinese children. It *does* mean that the white population of the Lower East Side in Manhattan makes almost no use of its public schools. Why? There are two substantial sections where whites live—one is Grand Street, the southernmost part of the district. The other is the area surrounding the Village View cooperative apartments. Grand Street is overwhelmingly Jewish, mostly elderly, and that part of its population which is not elderly sends its children to private, particularly Jewish, schools. However, this elderly Jewish population does have a stake in the public schools—its sons and daughters or grand-daughters or nieces and nephews are teachers and supervisors across the city. The other section, Village View, is populated by Catholic ethnics — Italians, Poles and Ukrainians — who use parochial schools.

By combining the racial fears of these two populations, the UFT has hand-picked and financed six virtually lilywhite slates of community school-board candidates since 1970. They have elected white majorities in each election. In 1973 and 1974 they ran with slates of eight whites and one black. In 1977, nine whites, no Puerto Ricans, no blacks. The one black candidate in 1973 was the brother of a special representative of the UFT on the union headquarters payroll.

Their literature, in high-priced, banner headlines, announced: "Stop Racism—Vote the Brotherhood Slate." They labelled the parent slate that opposed them as "separatist" and "racist," although it included blacks, Puerto Ricans, Chinese and whites. In their 1975 triumph, they got 6,000 votes from the Grand Street middle-income co-ops, which send less than 100 children to the district public schools. The Village View and Grand Street complexes accounted for over 80 percent of the vote total and all five of the candidates they elected lived in those two housing developments.

To maintain its control over the schools of District 1, the union used its influence to rig the election of 1973 in so blatant a way that a federal judge overturned its results.[2] The 1973 District 1 school-board elections were the first elections of any kind overturned on racial-discrimination grounds outside the states of Alabama and Louisiana.

In 1974 the union convinced an elderly Jewish population to vote in a school-board election where they had no direct interest by haunting them with their most fearful memories, by creating a kind of Hitler-like atmosphere, by thrusting me on the stage as the archetype anti-Semite, and by characterizing an entire parent population as grotesquely anti-Semitic. They got the white teachers of District 1 to finance and run a campaign against the very parent populations they must deal with daily. How do teachers face Puerto Rican parents, black parents, Chinese parents when with their money and their power they are saying that these parents are incapable of governing their schools?

The 1975 elections resulted in the largest turnout of black, Puerto Rican and Chinese voters in the five-year history of school decentralization. Our 1975 defeat cannot be attributed to the apathy of minority voters—they turned out at a greater rate per capita than white voters. The union's narrow, 5-4, victory was achieved by the simple fact that there are more white adults than the combined number of black, Chinese, and Puerto Rican adults.

Since June of 1975, the UFT majority has decimated the programs begun in District 1 on behalf of minority children — bilingual programs, black studies, reading programs, and the city's only decentralized food program. They have fired dozens of parent-selected minority and white professionals (Fuentes, 1976). They have returned the schools to the slumber the union enjoys in the other 30 decentralized school districts of the city.

The Transformation of the UFT

The union's reward for the wars it has made in Ocean Hill, Harlem, the Lower East Side and elsewhere is the ownership of the New York City school system. Shanker's personal rewards include a vice presidency of the AFL-CIO, the presidency of the AFT, dominance in statewide teacher and labor politics, and a future as a national labor leader. The political alliances that have resulted are most instructive; they illustrate the changing role of the UFT from a progressive to a conservative, reactionary, establishment organization. Consider these examples:

1. In 1970, Arthur Goldberg opposed Nelson Rockefeller for governor of New York. Goldberg, as a private attorney and later as U.S. Secretary of Labor, had been instrumental in founding the UFT

138

and gaining collective bargaining rights for it during the early sixties. On the other hand, each year of the Rockefeller administration had resulted in a reduction in the percentage of state aid to the total cost of New York City schools. Yet Shanker endorsed Rockefeller.

2. With a Republican-dominated state legislature, Shanker aligned the union with the most reactionary Republican-Conservatives in Albany. The union routinely endorsed State Senator John Marchi, together with a host of Republican-Conservatives. These individuals became the UFT pipeline for legislation in Albany.

3. In 1972, the AFT national convention voted to endorse George McGovern for president. The UFT used all its influence at the national level to block the endorsement. Failing that, they refused to contribute a dime and took a no-endorsement local position. Shanker's opposition to McGovern, stated in his weekly New York Times advertisement, was due to McGovern's support of affirmative action "quotas." Nixon, the beneficiary of the Shanker-Meany line, had vetoed more education legislation than any other president in American history. Less federal money for schools was not as important in Shanker's view as the horrifying potential of more jobs for blacks and Puerto Ricans.

4. In 1973, Shanker cemented his alliance with the regular Democratic organizations in New York City by becoming the major labor extension of the Beame mayoralty campaign.

5. In 1974 and 1976, the UFT endorsed almost every regular-organization candidate for local races in every borough of the city. The return of Tammany Hall to New York City governance was hailed by Shanker as a return to stability. In community school-board elections throughout the city, UFT slates have been combined with the clubhouse interests of regular Democratic organizations, particularly those of black and Puerto Rican politicians. The prototype of this phenomenon — the UFT alliance with Assemblyman Sam Wright's Democratic clubhouse school board in District 23 — was the pacification device that has narcotized the people of Ocean Hill since 1969 (Barrett, 1976).

To the degree that the union contains and represses the anticolonial instincts of the minority poor, that is the degree to which both the union and Shanker's own career profit and advance. But that does not necessarily mean that one caused the other, unless it is conceded that the practice of racism is the route to power in this society, that no truly progressive force ever prospers, that this is the essence of the reward system of American politics. Frantz Fanon (1967:85) has written:

> Once and for all I will state this principle: A given society is racist or it is not. . . Statements, for example, that the north of France is more racist than the south, that racism is the work of underlings and hence in no way involves the ruling class, that France is one of the least racist countries in the world are the product of men incapable of straight thinking.

If American society is racist, then to be a part of it, to share in its wealth, requires sharing its racism. Until 1968 the UFT was newborn, an unsettled question mark. Today it is a primary colonizing agent, rewarded in proportion to the domesticating power it exercises over our schools and communities. In this view, a kind of piggyback structure of American oppression emerges, with each layer atop the other, with Shanker's union atop the schools of the poor, manipulated by the layers atop it, particularly the corporate-governmental interests that determine its contract. And thus in this social structure that lives off the children at its bottom, teachers make more money not when they teach more effectively, but when they cease to teach at all and become the politicized instruments of racial stratification.[3]

The Struggle for Minority Children

In 1968 our movement in the schools crystallized all of the other, related pressures for liberation. We cannot accept the claim that it is only in periods of white prosperity that black and brown voices will be heard and that white recession forecloses our rights to a voice. They hear us when we make them listen.

This is the basic point I want to make: Activities in our minority communities are part of a movement, this movement survived the Great Racist Strikes of 1968, and it is now 11 years old. Our enemies in the media have distorted our movement by naming it after Rhody McCoy, Andrew Donaldson and even myself, but each of us has proven dispensable, because ours is a movement of people, not of leaders. It is a movement that survives because it expresses these thoughts of Frantz Fanon (1967:222):

I said. . .that man is a *yes*. I will never stop reiterating that. *Yes* to life. *Yes* to love. *Yes* to generosity. But man is also a *no*. *No* to scorn of man. *No* to degradation of man. *No* to exploitation of man. *No* to the butchery of what is most human in man: freedom.

This is what I mean by the union's transformation of our school system into an unbending public-works project: We grind out jobs. We dispense salaries. We help keep the economy fluid in Queens and the suburban counties. The schools exist for the people who work in them. The system churns on, an adult world living off children's needs but meeting the adult needs of the people who run it. Thus one can say that the New York public school system is the most successful in the world, that is, it pays the highest number of teachers the highest annual salaries. That has become its purpose.

Our actions are based on a single premise: the unions run these schools based upon what is best for their membership; it is time for the community to run these schools based upon what is best for its children. We are not talking nationalism or ethnic quotas. We are talking the sensible imposition of new priorities. Schools are for children and the jobs are to filled by those who can offer something to children. It is clear that we in the black and Puerto Rican communities must provide our own answers to our problems. But we must be aware that the institutions within our communities do not now belong to us. They don't because they mean too much in profits to absentee overlords such as these professional unions. Only struggle and perseverance will bring our institutions home to us.

NOTES

1. Decentralization refers to legislation in 1970 which redistributed the administrative control of the New York City school system at the top while delegating limited authority to smaller community units. Personnel matters, teacher contracts, curriculum and supportive services remained centrally controlled. During the 1960's the community clamored for control of its schools and the New York State Legislature responded with this law, which was supported by the UFT and the CSA.
2. Coalition for Education in District 1, et al. vs. Board of Elections of the City of New York, et al., SDCNY 370 F supp. 42 (1974); aff'd CANY 495 F 2d 1090 (1974).
3. See "N.Y.C. schools reading scores." New York Times, January 12, 1976.

REFERENCES

Barrett, Wayne. Albert Shanker, the U.F.T. and the New York City Schools. Unpublished manuscript. 1976.

Fanon, Frantz. Black Skin, White Masks. New York: Grove Press. 1967.

Fuentes, Luis. The Fight Against Racism in Our Schools. New York: Pathfinder Press. 1973.

"Community control never failed — It wasn't tried." Phi Delta Kappan, 57, 10 (June): 692-695. 1976.

New York City Civil Liberties Union. Burden of the Blame. New York: NYC Civil Liberties Union. 1970.

Puerto Rican Barrio Politics
in the United States

Introduction

This essay is among the first to chronicle the origins of the Young Lords Organization in New York from the insider perspective of a second generation Puerto Rican. Guzmán illuminates the radical politics of a generation that came of age in the mid-sixties and early seventies. They were influenced by the contradictions of American promises for upward mobility and militant movements intended to secure the civil rights of African and other American minorities. Guzmán outlines the anti-establishment Puerto Rican and Latino student organizations engendered by the struggles of the period, concentrating on the formation of the Young Lords, whose insurgent politics and ideology "captured the imagination for the coming generation."

Between 1969 and 1974, the Young Lords set an impressive agenda for community empowerment. After the initial takeover of a Methodist Church in Spanish Harlem, they set about to establish breakfast programs, clothing drives and health services, and offered classes in Puerto Rican history and culture for the children of the Barrio. The Lords succeeded in forcing the city to screen for tuberculosis and lead poisoning, undertake prison reforms and restructure the administration of Lincoln Hospital in the South Bronx.

Today, interest in the origins and role of the Young Lords, as well as other historical antecedents in the New York Puerto Rican past, continues to grow. Guzmán revisited the subject in a *Village Voice* (March 21, 1995, pp. 24-31), article entitled "My Life as a Revolutionary." A video is in production and several dissertations are in the research stage.

PUERTO RICAN BARRIO POLITICS IN THE UNITED STATES

by Pablo "Yoruba" Guzmán

Most observers agree that "official" statistics on Puerto Rican demographics within the United States are way off; the supposed total of 1.7 million persons of Puerto Rican birth or parentage is off perhaps by as much as 44 percent, or 750,000. There are of course two reasons for this: as is the case with Afro-Americans, Puerto Ricans in the ghetto (where most of us live) are grossly undercounted; and, as is common with all Latinos, officials are not yet sure of what a Puerto Rican *is*, for we "look" Chinese, black, "Indian," and European.

The most succinct expression of this phenomenon which comes to mind occurred after a New York Yankee baseball game in the South Bronx, when one of the Boston Red Sox fans, obviously a member of that group of Bostonians influential in preventing buses from integrating schools, remarked upon seeing a group of Puerto Rican teenagers: "What kahnd ah niggahs ahre yah?" Despite the New England cadences in which this question was couched, undoubtedly reminding the Puerto Rican group of those great friends of the *barrio*, the Kennedys, they recovered enough to involve the Bostonian and his friends in a rather hastily-convened seminar entitled "Semantics and Self-Defense in the South Bronx."

This speaks volumes about the nature of Puerto Rican politics in the United States. There is the ordained "official" way and the opposing *barrio* response to it. This contradictory duality permeates and colors all aspects of Puerto Rican political life, whether in Chicago or San Juan. For it springs from the central fact of Puerto Rican life, namely, that we are a colonized people.

Within the *barrio*'s politics, this duality reflects itself in the bat-

---

Mr. Pablo "Yoruba" Guzmán is a Correspondent for WCBS TV News in New York City.

tle between reform liberals and revolutionary activists for pre-eminence among *barrio* hearts and minds. Ah, the astute reader will say, but what is the significance of that fact, kind sir? Surely this has been the case with every, ah, shall we say *oppressed* minority — "minority?"—all right then, nationality, oppressed nationality in this country. Hasn't every ethnic group in America undergone its debate between reform and revolution, assimilation and separatism? I mean, look at Booker T. Washington vs. W.E.B. DuBois, or even Yellow Feather and Crazy Horse; it all parallels Albizu Campos and Muñoz Marín or Herman Badillo and the Young Lords, not to mention Martin Luther King and Malcolm X.

True, all true, dear reader and critic — up to a point. There is, however, one fact which distinguishes Latins from all other "colored" minorities, including blacks, and that is our overwhelming preponderance in the working class. Income is only one factor, but the 1970 census determined that 95 percent of all Puerto Ricans in the U.S. between 16 and 65 earn under $10,000 a year. Most of the remaining five percent earn less than $30,000 per year, which means they're living in some new *barrios*. Since there are over five million Puerto Ricans in the world, with three and a half million in Puerto Rico, this leaves over one and a half million residing in North American *barrios*.

Before we continue to explore the profundity of the enormous quantitative percentage in the working class which dominates Puerto Rican life — a percentage which far exceeds that of any other racial/ethnic group numbering at least a million in America — we should take a quick look at how that minimum of one and a half million Puerto Ricans got to the United States, including the 6,000 in Hawaii.

There are Puerto Ricans in every state in the union. Most came to the country from Puerto Rico by way of New York City and at least one million of the Puerto Ricans in the United States live in that city. We came in waves, arriving in greatest numbers between the Depression and Korean War years. That was the pioneer generation, the group which fought to establish a beachhead for the rest. Their children, part of the overall postwar baby boom, have dominated the shape of Puerto Rican politics since the late sixties; and since they, along with the rest of their generation, are having babies at a later age than their parents did, their demographic bulge will continue to dominate Puerto Rican affairs for many years.

145

The Second Generation

This second generation of Puerto Ricans in the States — my generation — has two characteristics of prime importance to distinguish itself: (1) it has been a most radical generation, at least during the period in which it came to adolescence, between 1965 and 1973; and (2) it is the group realizing America's "upward mobility" promise in greatest numbers (thus far). The principal political fact of second-generation Puerto Rican life is a push-pull contradiction: a native radicalism steeped in being children of the *barrio*, of workers and of Latino working-class culture; and an inculcated desire towards assimilation of postwar American consumer values, obtained as children of the broad 1950's American social landscape.

Mickey Mouse and *Noche Buena*; Santa Claus and *Santería*; *Salsa* and Rock and Soul; Betances and Lincoln — this is the living diaspora within which young Puerto Ricans were brought up. And so, as the rest of our generation in North America — indeed, across the western world — raised hell in the sixties, Puerto Rican youth marched right in step, forming organizations like the Young Lords, the Puerto Rican Socialist Party (PSP), *El Comité*, and the Puerto Rican Student's Union. Though this vanguard differed among itself tactically — and, in the case of the Lords and PSP, strategically — there were some essential points of unity:

— Puerto Ricans in the States were children of the forced migration from Puerto Rico;

— Puerto Ricans in the States were victims of racism in North America;

— Puerto Ricans were also victims of capitalist exploitation;

— A radical socialist alternative was the only viable program for Puerto Ricans;

— Any solution that did not include independence for Puerto Rico could only be half-baked.

Immediately, "traditional" *barrio* representatives were put on notice. The Herman Badillos of the world, daring as early-sixties reform Democrats, paled in comparison with the homegrown *barrio* radicals. Not only did the kids' politics make sense; they were, after all, our kids, Badillo and other establishment mouthpieces be damned.

This modern Puerto Rican movement in the States—for there did exist earlier Betances-era "support groups" and Albizu Campos Nationalist Party chapters—gained hegemony in the political thinking of most of the second generation. The ideas of the liberal reformists were considered of secondary interest. Students, upon whom the hopes of the preceding "pioneer generation" were pinned, were particularly active supporters of the radical movement. Thus, for the five years 1969-1973, a broad radical philosophy captured the imagination of most of the coming generation. *Barrio* politics, as a result, have been stamped for the foreseeable future with the mark of militancy; and, in turn, this affects whatever Puerto Rican component exists of North American politics.

Before examining the implications of the above, I shall delve further into what happened during those five key years. And I would like the reader to know that the author's views are necessarily subjective, though objectivity is sought, because he was a leader of one of the revolutionary groups — Minister of Information of the Young Lords Party, to be exact.

Lords and Socialists

The Young Lords represented one of two competing schools of thought and action in Puerto Rican radical ranks in the U.S. The other was represented by the *Movimiento Pro Independencia* (M.P.I.). By 1972 both organizations, as part of a deepening of the radical process, underwent name changes reflective of structural, ideological, and organizational changes: the Lords became the Puerto Rican Revolutionary Workers Organization and M.P.I. became the Puerto Rican Socialist Party (PSP). MPI/PSP was founded in Puerto Rico, which pretty much determined the nature of its works in the States; the Lords, with the exception of a disastrous, ill-conceived attempt at establishing two branches in Puerto Rico (March 1971 — July 1972), were primarily a U.S. operation. Needless to say, this difference of origin played a great role in maintaining a gap between the two groups.

That gap was exacerbated by the groups' differing ideologies. PSP had a political line which closely allied it to the Communist Party of Cuba, the Communist Party of the USA, and the Communist Party of the Soviet Union. In the eyes of the Lords, this was sacrilege. While the Lords had a policy of "critical support" towards the Cuban Revolution, its view of the Communist Party-USA was on a level with the Republican Party, and the Communist Party-Soviet Union was seen as the sometimes friendly, sometimes hostile, global competitor of U.S. Imperialism, Inc.

The Lords were created out of that late-sixties ferment which gave birth to the "New Left." One of the main characteristics of the "New Left" was its disdain for the "Old Left," and while this has been belittled of late, there were sound reasons why. Basically, the CP-USA had come under complete control of the Soviet Party; since the death of Stalin in 1953, the Soviet leadership restored capitalism in the U.S.S.R. under control of their elite state apparatus; abroad, Soviet policy had become one of competing with the US, particularly in the Third World, for "spheres of influence;" in the States, the American Party ceased to be a fighting body. The cutting edge for the world's revolutionaries became where you stood on the great debates over this Soviet turnabout, most vividly captured in polemics between the Soviet Central Committee versus China's Mao Tse-Tung and Albania's Enver Hoxha. The Lords loved Mao; PSP thought he and his followers were "infantile."

At this point the reader has every right to ask, "What the hell has this got to do with *barrio* politics?" Plenty, comrade, because the nature of how that general debate unfolded between the Lords (YLP) and PSP played a more decisive role in Puerto Rican affairs during those five years and their aftermath than the debate between the Radicals (PSP-YLP) and the Reformers (Badillo-Vélez). And *that* is an indication of just how strong revolutionary thoughts and actions were in the *barrio*.

The immediate ideological conflict these two opposing schools engaged in, of course, was around the question, "Whither Puerto Rico?" However, you could only go so far debating the socialist future of an island that had a way to go before achieving independence. More timely were the debates which involved organizing approaches.

Following the purely legalistic example of the CP-USA, PSP's organizing was conducted primarily around issues like "Bicentennial without Colonies," or in petitioning the UN to declare Puerto Rico a colony, or in leading *independentistas* to the ballot, or in exposés of government corruption, or in demonstrations in Washington. The

Lords, while not necessarily rejecting any single above-cited tactic as a tool, placed more emphasis on winning supporters to the *extra-legal* approach — taking over failed institutional symbols, fighting police in the streets, establishing survival programs, demonstrating in the *barrio*. The Lords were soon characterized by PSP as "infantile;" PSP was depicted by the Lords as "revisionist."

One of the mass results of the PSP-YLP organizing rivalry — which went on not only in New York, but also in Boston, Philadelphia, Chicago, Hartford, Bridgeport, Newark, Hoboken, Rochester, Buffalo, Cleveland, Detroit, and elsewhere — was that for the second generation the ballot box was pretty much rejected as a vehicle of change. An almost instinctive "apathy" is part of the reason why so many eligible Puerto Ricans in the States don't vote, or even register; but also at work is a conscious rejection of voting, a legacy of those five militant years. Only in the last year have some radical leaders in Philadelphia and New York begun seriously exploring the feasibility of winning limited gains through highly localized elections.

As that militant wave of "second generation-ists" matures, it has begun only now to make itself felt in *barrio* life. The re-appraisal of the ballot box is only one indicator; rank-and-file agitation in such areas of Puerto Rican labor concentration as the hospitals is another. Why was there a delay in the militants' progress after 1973? What happened in the five years between 1973-1978?

Winter in America

Simply put, PSP, the Lords, and their counterparts across the States became victims of what Gil Scott-Heron calls "Winter in America." It was the time of the Nixonian counter-offensive, a process actually begun with J. Edgar Hoover's COINTELPRO Program.[1] (The Puerto Rican movement in modern times in the U.S. began in 1969; COINTELPRO's Puerto Rican component, "Operation Chaos," began in *1966*.)

Winter in America was not the result only of external forces; internally, we were, after all, young and prone to childish mistakes — like pointing the finger at each other, like indulging in sectarianism when ranks should have been tightened, like dogmatically applying theory, whether it "fit" or not, onto immediate practical situations.

We made mistakes; our ranks were infiltrated. Opportunists and police agents seized upon our errors and gradually our organizations moved away from what they started out to be. Rather than maintaining ourselves deeply in the midst of our people, providing living leadership, we grew more rhetorical, isolated, and ultimately passé. A new generation, barely five years younger than we, came into adolescence practically untouched by our words and almost ignorant of our deeds, for no new deeds were forthcoming. Many left the ranks; leaders were jailed; cynicism and mistrust set in. It was a time to find your own way, quietly.

Into this vacuum came the reformists, who were not really able to capture the popular imagination, but who regained control of *barrio* politics, making it strictly establishment politics once again. The mass fancy was caught instead by the new *Salsa* entrepreneurs, petty and would-be capitalists. One or two were "outsiders," i.e., Italian or Jewish; but by and large the work was done by *barrio* residents.

In age and style, this group was part of the same second generation which produced the militants. Indeed, a few were ex-militants. They used the movement's nationalist rhetoric to move *barrio* consumers. *Salsa* became the new movement, and the militants of old, who once had the opportunity to guide it but rejected it as beneath their political dignity, found themselves largely reduced to leafletting outside it. Once again a great truth of organizing was driven home to the would-be organizer: "If you can't hang out, you can't spread the word." Or: "Why should I listen to your politics? You can't even dance."

The last year, 1978-1979, has given rise to some interesting and hopeful signs. For one thing, five years of partying has taken its toll on the younger generation, who are not so easily conned by cries of "*Salsa!*,"especially now that they've begun paying their own rent. For another, second-generation militants have started coming out of their funk, and begun communicating. The realization that so many of us are now teachers, daycare workers, government clerks, ambulance drivers, lawyers, hospital workers, bank tellers, writers, janitors, and doctors has begun sinking in. The possibilities are intriguing, rooted in the fact that since 1969 things have gotten worse: the Bakke decision; FALN grand juries and police raids in Chicago and New York aimed not at terrorists but at everyone left of center;

150

unemployment and inflation; cutbacks of Puerto Rican studies programs; an end to college open enrollment; increased police brutality,
including "perfect (unsolved) murders," in the *barrio;* decreased
housing opportunities; closings of municipal hospitals. Finally, Puerto
Rico is still not free to govern its own affairs, as the ongoing fight of
the Vieques fishermen shows.

So the immediate future shows signs of learning from the immediate past; of a renewed, mature militancy forming in the *barrios*
to confront reform and opportunism in the eighties. Already, the
Puerto Rican Alliance in Philadelphia is setting an example for many.
Three of the four components of this grass-roots umbrella of seven
barrio community groups deal with housing, education, and police
brutality. The fourth gives support to the people of Vieques. In open
convention at their founding in March, 1979, the two principal leaders
elected — the only Puerto Ricans elected to anything in Philly —
happened to be former Young Lord leaders.

Winter, in the *barrios* of North America, is becoming Spring.
Again.

NOTE

1. COINTELPRO is an "intelligence community" acronym for COunter
   INTELligence PROgram. It was set up within the FBI during the last
   decade of J. Edgar Hoover's reign, in the mid-sixties. Originally, "scen-
   arios" planned as part of COINTELPRO operations were designed to
   subvert the black civil rights movement. But as radical social activism
   spread from southern black organizations to groups of all colors across the
   country, so too did the scope of COINTELPRO activities. "Operation
   Chaos" was a COINTELPRO subdivision for Puerto Rican radicals.

Puerto Rican Struggles in the Catholic Church

Introduction

In the years since the publication of this article, there has been an effusion of interest in the popular and institutional religious experiences of Puerto Ricans and other Latino/ Hispanics in the U.S. As an historically important mainland population that bridges urban continental diaspora communities with the Hispanic Caribbean, the Puerto Rican experience has been, and continues to be, notable in shaping the discourse.

The historical trajectory employed by Stevens-Arroyo in this seminal essay found broader articulation in works like *Oxcart Catholicism on Fifth Avenue* (1993), by Ana María Díaz Stevens, and the second edition of *Puerto Rican Americans: The Meaning of Migration to the Mainland* (1987), by Joseph Fitzpatrick. More recently, new issues, dimensions and methodologies have evolved in the literature on Latino religious studies.

As the focus on Puerto Rican religiosity expands to include non-Catholic denominations, research on the role of the Church and spirituality among Puerto Ricans and other Latinos has been similarly elaborated. Current trends in the research incorporate considerations that bring new understanding to the Puerto Rican experience. They include a broader, more comprehensive Latino contextual framework; perspectives on the relationship between the U.S. Latino religious experience and practices in their countries of origin; and innovative interpretations on the role of women in ministry.

The significant growth of the Latino/Hispanic population in the United States, augmented by an unprecedented increase in Caribbean, Central and South American immigration, positions the group influentially with regard to U.S. Christian beliefs and practices. The work initiated by Stevens-Arroyo in this volume opened new ground. It finds resonance in the research agenda of The Program for Analysis of Religion Among Latinos (PARAL), an interdisciplinary social science network that promotes the study of religious experience among the peoples of Latin American heritage, living in the United States and Puerto Rico.

PARAL has advanced the field through scholarship (Stevens-Arroyo, 1994) that explores cultural attitudes towards family, gender and community; Latino identity formation; the impact of Protestantism, Catholicism, feminism, nationalism and political activism on U.S. Latinos and Puerto Ricans; theories of syncretism; African and Indigenous influences upon Latino beliefs and practices; historical aspects of Cuban religion and the relationship of Santería to Gnosticism and Theosophy.

Finally, the research of the nineties significantly breaks gender barriers and sheds light on feminist theology within the context of Christian ministry. The role of Puerto Rican and other Latinas in a myriad of religious domains, as lay persons, ministers, nuns and providers of pastoral services, is at the core of work by María E. Pérez y González (1993), Ana María Díaz Stevens (1993), Ada María Isasi-Díaz and Yolanda Tarango (1988), Loida I. Martell Otero (1994), and Virginia Sánchez Korrol (1993).

PUERTO RICAN STRUGGLES IN THE CATHOLIC CHURCH

by Antonio M. Stevens-Arroyo

The strategies of service and outreach by the Catholic Church to the Puerto Ricans who have migrated to the United States in great numbers are of two types: first, massive assistance in socioeconomic terms, such as job-placement, education, better housing, etc.; and second, a method of evangelization which recognizes the cultural autonomy of a people who have no permanent loyalty to life in the United States, but are not necessarily hostile to North American ideals. The first set of priorities can be defined as "social action" and the second as "pastoral care."

The struggle of the Catholic Church of New York and the Northeast to understand these realities and to meet the needs they have created, along with the challenges to the Church's own structures and interests, constitutes the saga of the Spanish-speaking Apostolate.

Development of Spanish Apostolate in the Northeast

The Spanish Apostolate Office of the Archdiocese of New York must be the focus for any historical account of the pastoral care of the Church of the Northeast towards Puerto Ricans (Stevens-Arroyo, 1974: 119-130). There are three basic reasons for this. Firstly, the Archdiocese, which includes the boroughs of Manhattan and the Bronx, was the initial focus of the heaviest migration from the island. Secondly, the size, wealth and prestige of New York automatically place the Archdiocese in a role of pastoral leadership. Thirdly, since New York City has a reputation for liberal and innovative social

Dr. Antonio M. Stevens-Arroyo is Professor of Puerto Rican Studies, Brooklyn College, City University of New York, Brooklyn, N.Y.

welfare and educational programs, the Archdiocese had opportunities to politically develop the Puerto Rican constituency, which is overwhelmingly Catholic, thus turning them into a powerful ethnic Catholic voting block. This third point is an important one, since it implies that both the city fathers and churchmen expected a pattern of cultural assimilation for Puerto Ricans that had been the process for other immigrant groups to New York. It was hoped that the Catholic Church would organize the Puerto Rican community the way that the synagogue had pulled together the Jewish immigrants and black Baptist Churches had stabilized the migration from the South. In other words, Puerto Ricans were expected to follow the well-worn path to Americanization that had been taken by the Irish, Italians, Hungarians, Poles and so forth (Fitzpatrick, 1972).

The efforts of the Church to achieve this assimilation of Puerto Ricans to the dominant North American value system was channeled through the institutions of the church: parish church, parochial school, Catholic charities, etc.; as well as the influence of the Church elite, i.e., the clergy and religious women or sisters. Through these means the Catholic Church of the United States had linked together religion and nationality as a part of the process of Americanizing self-identification. In the words of Andrew Greeley (1972: 125): "as the young person is socialized within his religio-ethnic group, he thinks of himself not so much as a Catholic, but as a Polish Catholic, Irish Catholic, Italian Catholic, French Catholic, thus distinguishing himself not only from Protestants but also from Catholics of other ethnic backgrounds."

It is the thesis of Patrick H. McNamara of the University of New Mexico that neither the institutional nor the clerical elite of the Catholic Church produced this kind of ethnic Catholicism for the Mexican Americans of the United States (McNamara, 1973: 124-130; 1970: 449-485). The same would seem to be true for the Puerto Ricans, particularly those in New York City and the Northeastern United States.

In the model for development and eventual incorporation into the mainstream of New York City life and politics, the settlement house was an important ingredient. By providing essential social services to the poor migrant, charity propped up the immigrant community until employment and education made it self-supporting. As far back as 1934, influential Catholic laypersons had helped launch *Casita María* in East Harlem, a settlement house in the long New York immigrant tradition. Strongly identified with Sr. Carmelita, a Puerto Rican Trinitarian sister, the *Casita* was later moved to the Bronx. On the Lower East Side, the Jesuits founded Nativity Mission Center, which was to be shaped in its thrust by the tireless efforts of the Puerto Rican Fr. Walter Janer, who remained as director through most of the years 1953-1964. However, the role of the settlement houses was more important to the Protestant work among Puerto Ricans than it was for the Catholic Church (Ribes Tovar, 1970: 236; Wakefield, 1959).

The immediate preoccupation of Cardinal Spellman in New York was pastoral care, i.e., the religious practice of the Puerto Ricans. Although the Cardinal had abandoned the small national parish as a means of evangelizing the Puerto Ricans and had attempted to integrate pastoral care for the Spanish-speaking into the territorial parishes, the increasing numbers of Puerto Rican migrants outdistanced these measures (Fitzpatrick, 1971: 125 ff.). A survey in 1949 showed that 50 percent of Puerto Ricans married in New York that year were united in Protestant ceremonies, as contrasted with only 14.3 percent in Puerto Rico. In the Catholic rite, the proportion was reversed, with the island Church attracting 61.4 percent of marriages, while in the city only 27 percent of Puerto Ricans were married as Catholics (Fitzpatrick, 1971: 93). In other words, a great number of Puerto Ricans in New York were leaving the Catholic religion to be married in Protestant ceremonies, and 70 percent or more of these Protestants were Pentecostals (O'Dea and Poblete, 1960: 18-36). This appalling statistic prompted the Cardinal to entrust Msgr. Joseph Connolly with a mission of coordinating parish efforts at a diocesan level, and to begin preparing New York priests to work with Puerto Ricans by learning Spanish as the Redemptorist missionaries were doing.

These initial efforts clearly correspond to the models of "social action" and "pastoral care" as were then current within Catholic circles. But the character of the social help from the settlement houses was largely paternalistic and, as in the case of St. Cecilia's Parish, did not count upon a native Puerto Rican clerical elite. Hence, while these programs certainly attracted larger numbers of Puerto Ricans to the Catholic Church, they did not function to socialize the new arrivals into the familiar ethnic Catholicism model. Without native Puerto Rican leadership as priests, the paternalism of the

157

Catholic programs of that time weakened, rather than strengthened, the ethnic identification of Puerto Ricans in the United States.

In 1953, at the urging of the Yugoslavian-born Ivan Illich and Father Joseph Fitzpatrick from Fordham University, the Archdiocese instituted the San Juan Fiesta. This celebration was highlighted by a public mass and sermon; in 1956 it was transferred to Downing Stadium in Randall's Island, where the event attracted a yearly attendance of some 50,000 or more Puerto Ricans.

The San Juan Fiesta was successful largely because it met a need of the rapidly growing Puerto Rican community for a mass event of socio-cultural identification. At that time, there was no Puerto Rican Day Parade, no Folklore Festival and very little political or cultural visibility by Puerto Ricans in the city. This effort to alter the pattern of institutional relationships with the Puerto Rican was complemented by a program designed to train the clerical elites to the new purpose. In 1957, Msgr. Illich departed for Puerto Rico to initiate a school for clergy in order to have them assimilate to the Puerto Ricans in their parishes rather than vice-versa.

The Intercultural Institute was conducted during the summer months in Ponce, Puerto Rico, and the programs of language training were heavily supplemented by strong doses of field experience. This missionary approach to the training of diocesan clergy within the United States was ahead of its time. Indeed, the later organization of Illich's Cuernavaca establishment, the *Centro Intercultural de Documentación* (CIDOC), and the Mexican American Cultural Center (MACC) in San Antonio, Texas, owe very much to the Intercultural Institute founded by the Archdiocese of New York.

Although the Institute attracted participants from all over the country, and helped train church personnel destined for work in Latin America and with Chicanos as well as Puerto Ricans in the United States, the presence of Archdiocesan clergy characterized its thrust. Such large numbers of newly-ordained priests attended the sessions that it was, for all practical purposes, an extension of the seminary for many years.

The clergy who entered into the Institute under the direction of Msgr. Illich were among the most dedicated, highly motivated and active of the New York priests. It can be stated that the Archdiocese gave its richest resources to the Puerto Rican people. This gift was not one of buildings or grants of money alone, but rather a heavy investment in personnel. It would be difficult to find a diocese which responded as quickly or as totally to a new pastoral need in the twentieth century as did the Archdiocese of New York to the Puerto Rican people in the first decade of the Spanish Catholic Action Office.

The Cursillo Movement

In 1960, Msgr. James Wilson, who in 1956 had replaced the ailing Msgr. Connolly as Director of the Spanish Catholic Action Office, launched the *Cursillo* movement from the Archdiocesan office. The *Cursillo de Cristiandad* is a spiritual renewal movement within the Catholic Church that came from Spain to the U.S. in 1960. It is a weekend retreat where the faith of the Christian believer is re-awakened through a series of talks delivered by lay persons, many without formal theological training. The purpose of this intensive program of Christian formation was to prepare lay persons — in this case, Puerto Ricans — for a role in the apostolate. For this program, the Augustinian Recollect Fathers were contracted to direct formation and St. Joseph's *Cursillo* Center was opened on the West Side of Manhattan on 145th Street between Broadway and Amsterdam Avenue. The *Cursillo* movement enjoyed spectacular success, and the movement sprang up in the ensuing years in Brooklyn, Newark, Philadelphia and a number of New England dioceses.[1] In practically every case, the pattern of development was similar: first, the *Cursillo* movement was introduced by a team from outside the diocese after some of them had traveled to another place where it had already been initiated; secondly, the official diocesan response was to assign a Spanish-speaking priest as Director, very often a member of a religious order from Spain; thirdly, the Spanish-speaking membership became so numerous that in the Puerto Rican community to be a *Cursillista* and a Catholic was almost one and the same thing.

The *Cursillo* movement went beyond the San Juan Fiesta in meeting the needs of the Puerto Rican community in several ways:

(1) It provided not a one-day, but a year-round involvement in an institutional framework of high prestige for the migrant.
(2) The moral conversion of the *Cursillo* and its tightly-knit *ultreya* (follow-up) system invoked peer pressure on individual behavior,

and since the *Cursillo* demanded more than a cultural practice of Catholicism, it produced solidly-grounded leadership. Only those who were living according to Church marriage laws, with stable family relationships and socially acceptable behavior could become influential in the movement.

(3) The ideals of the *Cursillo* movement encouraged lay initiative and participation, which compensated in part for the absence of a native clergy. Sometimes, when the Spanish-speaking curate was not integrated into the parochial staff, the leadership of the *Cursillo* movement in a local church became a parish-within-a-parish.

These factors served to make the *Cursillo* movement the point of cultural identification of the Puerto Rican with Catholicism, but what the movement lacked was integration of the cultural process into the social welfare dimensions of the pastoral efforts of the Church. This deficiency was to become more evident as the changes of the Second Vatican Council drastically changed the meaning of social action.

Summer in the City: 1964-1969

In 1963 the dynamic and charismatic Robert Fox assumed the directorship of the Spanish Catholic Action Office. His entry coincided with significant trends in the Church and the world. The Second Vatican Council recast the liturgy, sacramental system and ecclesiology of the Church. The Civil Rights movement and its products, the War on Poverty and Black Power militancy, altered substantially the tenor of life in a ghetto neighborhood. Finally, the urban-renewal programs, with the towering public-housing projects that they spawned, destroyed much of the cohesiveness of local communities. Charity now had to be organized into grantsmanship, involving much paper work and a continual search for funding sources.

Msgr. Fox sought to bring together the Church's commitment to the Puerto Rican community with the resources available through government agencies. The new program he created was called Summer in the City, but it was destined to clash with the established values of the Catholic Church. Because the new approach attempted to fuse together concern for social development with the pastoral or ecclesiastical needs of Puerto Ricans, it challenged the validity of the more established patterns for ethnic Catholic assimilation into North

American society. Fox's administration had the misfortune of coinciding with the administration of Mayor Lindsay in New York City, and the marginalization of "ethnic groups," such as the Irish and the Italians in favor of the "minority groups," such as the blacks and Puerto Ricans. Thus, Msgr. Fox found it impossible to mobilize the Church hierarchy around the new movement putting down roots among Puerto Rican Catholics.

The Office of the Spanish Apostolate: 1969-1973

Father Robert Stern became the head of the Spanish Catholic Action Office in 1969. Not a charismatic leader for social causes like his predecessor, Stern's background in the Chancery and studies in Canon Law prepared him best for the administrative aspects of his new post. His personal simplicity of life and quiet manner, however, earned him the respect of the activist clergy. Stern set out to structure and reorganize the different elements of the Hispanic community so as to make his office an "umbrella" under which other movements would be coordinated and could grow. He strengthened the approach of Fox, who had fused together social and pastoral needs, by adding Puerto Ricans to the staff of his office[2] and by democratizing all the Church structures under his administration. Perhaps the most important of his innovations was the key role he played in organizing the First National Hispano Pastoral *Encuentro*, which was held in Washington, D.C. in June of 1972. This was intended as a meeting of Chicanos, Puerto Ricans and Cubans within the Church who wished more services in the style of "minority groups" from the bishops of the country. In preparation for the national meeting, Stern decided to hold a series of local assemblies and workshops to solidify the New York delegation. He chose a format suggested by Father Edgard Beltrán, a priest from Colombia, skilled in adult education in the combined social-pastoral approach later to become known as "The Theology of Liberation."

The Archdiocesan *Encuentros* directed by Fr. Beltrán[3] served to raise the level of expectations of Puerto Rican Catholics; they began to believe that they could expect a greater openness from the Cardinal and his intimate advisors. However, the tone of the *Encuentros* was one of debate and dialogue, an approach foreign to the mode of operation then acceptable to the Chancery. The Rubicon was crossed when a delegation of some 17 persons, selected from among those who had participated in the *Encuentros*, wrote on March 13, 1972 to Cardinal Cooke, asking for an interview. The letter detailed the needs of the Hispanic people and asked for greater Hispanic representation at all levels of Archdiocesan decision-making. There were four specific recommendations:

(1) The naming of an Episcopal Vicar for the Spanish-speaking.
(2) The naming of a Vicar General who spoke Spanish.
(3) Direct collaboration with the Coordinating Committee.
(4) The ordination of a Hispanic as auxiliary bishop.

The meeting took place on March 29, 1972. And apparently, since the process of mutual decision that Fr. Stern had initiated was not fully understood by the Cardinal and his representatives, there were undeniable tensions in the air.[4] There never was a second meeting, and no immediate action. The success of the National *Encuentro*, however, served to increase rather than diminish fears in official Chancery circles. They found unacceptable the policies which directed church institutions and clerical elites to new purposes of social and pastoral development under democratic structures and native Puerto Rican leadership. Father Stern resigned his post in February of 1973 and was succeeded by an Irish priest who did not continue these policies (New York Daily News, 2/18/1973). After a series of confrontations between frustrated Puerto Rican leaders and proponents of the hard-line Chancery stand,[5] including the summary dismissal of the only Puerto Rican priest left in the Spanish-speaking Office (New York Daily News, 4/19/1973), Father Joaquín Beaumont, a European-born Basque, was named to much reduced co-responsibilities with the previously-appointed Father Francis X. Gorman (New York Daily News, 8/23/1973). This pattern, which continued with the appointment of Father Ignacio Lazcano, another Basque who succeeded Father Beaumont in 1976, apparently represents the acquiescence of the New York hierarchy to the modernizing fusion of social action with pastoral care.

This new era, which began in 1973, has four clear distinguishing marks. Firstly, being Hispanic by birth is a requisite for leadership. North American priests who speak Spanish are less important than before: Hispanic priests and lay persons have more to say in policy. Secondly, the number of other Hispanic migrants, such as Dominicans, Colombians, Ecuadorians and Cubans, now makes it impossible to speak of "Puerto Ricans" as if they represented all the Spanish-speaking population. Thirdly, consolidation, centralization, and the formation of "centers," replace much of the parish orientation of the past, as well as Chancery-based offices. Fourthly, there is competition for legitimacy among those who (1) emphasize cultural independence of Hispanos from Anglos, (2) those who stress political power within present political structures, and (3) those who emphasize a radical change in socio-economic reality through collective action.

Cultural independence, which emphasizes language, customs and folklore as the means for Puerto Rican identification with the Church, has as a principal source of diffusion the Northeast Regional Pastoral Center for Hispanics, which was opened in April of 1976. The Association of Hispanic Priests (ASH) and, more recently, Padres of the Apostolate of the Northeast (PAN) are clerical groups which reflect this general approach to matching social with pastoral activity under the direction of Hispanics. The second group, which fosters Puerto Rican development within present political structures, has produced Father Louis Gigante, an Italian priest-politician for the South Bronx, and a host of other clerics who serve on various neighborhood boards representing the Puerto Ricans in their parishes. Finally, there are those who have opted for a liberationist ideology, such as Christians for Socialism, The Alternative Coalition (TAC) and the youth group, *Naborí*. These latter are consonant with the goals of PADRES, a Chicano priest organization very influential in the Southwest and Texas.

None of these ideologies has yet been completely successful in capturing the loyalties of Puerto Rican Catholics in New York City and the Northeast. Recent years have seen an accelerating alienation from established Church structures. On the one hand, there is a millenarian-type movement called "Catholic Pentecostalism" or "Catholic Charismatics," which is sociologically identical with the storefront Protestant Pentecostals described by O'Dea and Poblete (1960). Secularism is also on the increase, while growing numbers of young Puerto Ricans are turning to forms of *Espiritismo*, an eclectic mix of African and Catholic beliefs, to satisfy religious instincts. These mystical, at times magical, cults coexist with a rejection of traditional beliefs of Catholicism and an acceptance of a secular rationalist world-view. It would seem that because the Catholic

Church in the United States has never fostered a sense of ethnic Catholicism among Puerto Ricans in their socialization patterns, Church influence in areas such as New York City, where Puerto Ricans are the largest Catholic group, will be weak. On the other hand, the religious fervor of Puerto Ricans should produce new strategies of social and pastoral activity, as official Church leaders make adaptations in order to maintain credibility as the traditional faith of Puerto Ricans.

NOTES

1. Brooklyn's *Cursillos* begin in December 1962, with the Center opened in 1963. Newark's began in 1964, as did Philadelphia's.
2. The priests of Puerto Rican ancestry were Frs. José McCarthy-González, OFM, Cap. Luis Ríos, AA, and Antonio Stevens-Arroyo, CP. These were later joined by César Ramírez.
3. The *Encuentros* were held on September 24-26 and October 9, 1971; also on January 8, 1972.
4. Participants in the meeting were: Cardinal Cooke, Bishop Head, Msgr. Mahoney, Msgr. O'Keefe and Msgr. Kenny. The commission included Frs. Neil Grahman, José McCarthy-González and José Viana; Mr. Edward Kalbfleish, Luis Fontanez, José Sosa, Pedro Santiago, Gloria Román, Cándida Solá, Cristina Santos and Haydée Burges. Stern was also present.
5. "Protesters Here Say Archdiocese Ignores Needs of Hispanic Groups," New York Times, March 29, 1973, p. 15; "Charge Cooke with Neglect of Hispanics," Daily News, March 29, 1973, p. 61. The protesters also presented a memorandum from Stern to the Vicar General, dated March 24, 1972, and the Three Year Report of the Spanish-speaking Apostolate, 1969-1972. The event was filmed and a story shown by WCBS-TV; somewhat later a film story was presented on Public Television, and a story on "The Irish Connection," by Robert Sam Anson, appeared in The New Times, May 17, 1974, pp. 29-33.

REFERENCES

Fitzpatrick, Joseph P. Puerto Rican Americans: The Meaning of Migration to the Mainland. Englewood Cliffs, New Jersey: Prentice-Hall. 1971.

"The Role of the National Parish and the Puerto Rican Experience." Clergy Report 2, 6 (June). 1972.

Greeley, Andrew M. The Denominational Society: A Sociological Approach to Religion in America. Glenview, Illinois: Scott, Foresman. 1972.

McNamara, Patrick. "Dynamics of the Catholic Church: From Pastoral to Social Concern," in Leo Grebler, Joan W. Moore, and Ralph Guzmán, eds., The Mexican American People. New York: Macmillan-Free Press. 1970.

"Catholicism, Assimilation, and the Chicano Movement: Los Angeles as a Case Study," in Rudolph de la Garza, Anthony Kruszewski, Thomas Arciniega, eds., Chicanos and Native Americans. Englewood Cliffs, New Jersey: Prentice-Hall. 1973.

O'Dea, Thomas and René Poblete. "Anomie and the quest for community: The formation of sects among Puerto Ricans in New York." American Catholic Sociological Review, 21 (Spring): 18-36. 1960.

Ribes Tovar, Federico. El Libro Puertorriqueño de Nueva York. New York: Plus Ultra. 1970.

Stevens-Arroyo, Antonio M. "Religion and the Puerto Ricans in New York," in Edward Mapp, ed., Puerto Rican Perspectives. Metuchen, N.J.: Scarecrow Press. 1974.

Wakefield, Dan. Island in the City: The World of Spanish Harlem. Boston: Houghton Mifflin. 1959.

Puerto Rican Spiritualism: Survival of the Spirit

Introduction

This last article on spiritualism is similar to many of the others in this collection in that it was written at a time when there was little interest or sympathy—indeed, in some cases there was antipathy—for the views expounded. Some viewed spiritualism as part of Puerto Ricans' and other Latinos' bizarre cultural practices. However, as this article made clear, and as others came to acknowledge, spiritualism was a culturally sanctioned method of treating emotional difficulties and traumas. In some ways, it was more effective than the traditional methods in use at the time.

For example, it did not stigmatize individuals as "mentally ill." It provided culturally-sanctioned support during periods of stress and a means whereby emotional issues were discussed and addressed in Spanish—without fear of long-term institutionalization in state mental hospitals.[1] This article highlighted how spiritualism provided an accepting, culturally sanctioned atmosphere, to which a patient could resort and within which the client's value system was not replaced by that of the therapist.

The article by Franklyn Sánchez was novel because it focused on the similarities between psychotherapeutic techniques and spiritist practice, and it illustrated the advantages (for some) of the spiritualist's approach. For example, it pointed out the similarities that existed between the id-ego-super-ego concepts and spiritualism's concepts of "espíritus malos-guías-protección" (bad spirits-guides-and good spirits). The article also stressed the similarities between the goals of psychotherapy and spiritism. Moreover, it showed how the spiritist expanded the person's self awareness and ego-strength without entering into a personalized or negative relationship with the patient. The article argued that the externalization of negative feelings via external spiritual forces helped patients to better confront the subjective realm. This allowed the patient to deflect usual feelings of anger, hostility or love that often evolve toward therapists in traditional psychotherapeutic relationships.

Also clarified in this article was how the spiritualist's use of "objects of faith" served as means by which the client actively and positively participated in the process of "getting better." These "objects of faith" provided ego strengthening, giving the wearer a sense of confidence that helped her or him to deal with adversity more positively and directly. The fact that the objects were often individualized made their significance and perceived assistance greater. However, the article made clear that praying to the spirits, lighting candles, wearing objects, and herb baths were seen as adjuncts to, not substitutes for, the patient's own strength. Part of the spiritist's role was to help the patient to accept responsibility. A case history illustrated these points.

Note

1. Unfortunately, a substantial but never-officially-ascertained number of Spanish-speaking patients became needlessly and endlessly embroiled in the early mental health system. This occurred when they were diagnosed as "schizophrenic" for what might have been culturally appropriate behavior. For example, a Puerto Rican women experiencing an "ataque de nervios" (attack of nerves) during a stressful time might appear to be having a bizarre psychotic episode, which would necessitate institutional treatment (Guarnaccio, De La Cancela, and Carrillo, 1989). The lack of Spanish-speaking personnel and the policy of long-term institutional care meant that many were not able "fly over the cuckoo's nest." Much psychological damage, some lobotomies, and drug-inflicted damage, e.g., from strong tranquilizers, occurred in these cases.

PUERTO RICAN SPIRITUALISM:
SURVIVAL OF THE SPIRIT

by Franklyn D. Sánchez

Spiritism[1] is the belief in the world of spirits. Beginning with the Christian precept that the human soul is immortal, spiritism contends that the world of the dead continues to interact with the world of the living. Although belief in the existence of the soul is found in practically all cultures, spiritism as a belief system was not codified until Hippolyte O. Rivail, alias Allan Kardec, a French adept, wrote three major books on the subject in the late 1850's.

Through translation, the work of Kardec reached Puerto Rico. It was brought there by upper-class Puerto Ricans in the nineteenth century. Today many well-known lawyers, doctors, senators, artists and poets are adherents of spiritism. In fact, one of the best-known and respected poets of contemporary Puerto Rico, Francisco Matos Paoli, is an acknowledged practitioner who established a flourishing temple in his home town. As with most cultural phenomena, the system eventually filtered toward the poor of the island. It has been commonly accepted that although officially Puerto Ricans may be Catholic or Protestant, many also practice spiritism.

Spiritism, basically, assigns many interpersonal and intra-psychic emotional problems to the presence of a spirit who is bent on tormenting its victim. Briefly, spiritism posits that the spirits of the dead or disincarnated spirits can communicate with an incarnated spirit, or one which occupies a living body, through a medium or person who has developed the special ability to work with and manage them. The disincarnated spirit is chained to an irrevocable law of evolution divinely planned. Basically, this is the concept of metempsychosis. Eventually, it progresses through three levels and ten

Mr. Franklyn D. Sánchez continues his counseling practice and is also Principal of an Intermediate School in the Bronx.

grades until it becomes enlightened and refined. While it is evolving, the spirit goes through "tests." These tests are responsible for the mental and physical anguish which the afflicted person feels. Everything from excessive drinking to homicidal and suicidal behavior to feelings of depersonalization and marital strife is attributed to the spirits.

There are those, like Dr. Vivian Garrison (1972), who argue convincingly that there are similarities between the therapeutic techniques of the mental-health professional and the procedures employed by the spiritist. I can see such parallels also.

Psychotherapeutic Technique and Spiritist Practice

Buscando la causa, or identifying the spiritual cause of the affliction, is analogous to the initial interview in therapy. The working through of a given problem is similar to the spiritist's *trabajando la causa*, or working with the spirits. The cleansing and ritual purification which the spiritist performs is much like the closure of *Gestalt* which the patient achieves in treatment. The development of *facultades*, of the patient's spiritual powers, or the ability to manage the forces of the spirit, is not unlike the carryover patients experience after the successful reorganization of the balance of *id-ego-superego* impulses. Even dream interpretation and the elucidation of symbols by the therapist is very much like the interpretation of "evidences" or visions which the spiritist shares with the patient. Both practitioners interpret non-verbal language as a *cue* to the patient's affliction. Termination is based upon the patient's having learned sufficient coping skills. Thus, the aims of the spiritualist and therapist are identical. The major difference in terms of technique is that the spiritualist brings the answer to the patient and "foretells" the problem, whereas the therapist waits for the patient to reveal his problem and times his interpretations.

However, most mental-health professionals I have interviewed continue to treat patients who experience and share spiritualist phenomena with them as hysterics. Apart from its religious significance, the practice of spiritism often brings relief from emotional problems. For many practitioners, good health was traditionally framed in terms of the absence of psychological conflict which paralyzed or seriously interfered with normal interpersonal relations between the client and others. However, with the growth of psychotherapy, most practitioners now have expanded their philosophical outlook. Not only is absence of conflict important, but evidence of positive emotional growth in which the potential of the client is creatively explored is now stressed. Along with this concern, therapists understand that a human being is embedded in the culture in which he was born. As a result, certain images and certain ways of behaving and beliefs inherent in that culture are passed on to him early in life. In his work with patients, the psychotherapist must be aware of these culturally unique reactions and use them as vehicles whenever possible to establish a trusting relationship with the clients.

It has been my experience that people who see spiritists may eventually consult a clinician as well. The efficacy of treatment really depends upon the faith quotient of the client. If the client believes that the system works, then it does. A number of spiritists have formed relationships with medical doctors. A spiritist I know routinely refers her clients to a doctor who does a thorough medical work-up to determine whether the patient's ailment has any organic base. If no physical cause is discovered, then the spiritist will see the client.

In my psychoanalytic work with Puerto Rican patients, I find that even the most sophisticated will at first omit to mention their belief or contact with spiritism, although they report that their parents are heavily involved in following spiritist practices to the letter. My clients, on the other hand, claim to rely on their parents' prayers. They admit eventually to consulting a spiritist only at specified times of stress.

Objects of Faith

The spiritist system with its use of cards, potions, amulets, etc. provides innumerable concrete "objects of faith" that serve as (different) means by which the client actively and positively participates in the process of "getting better." These objects of faith are helpful and convenient pegs upon which to hang one's emotions, hopes, illusions, desires, fantasies, goals. The wearing of a spiritist's necklace, for example, provides ego-strengthening assurance that no harm will come to the wearer. With such a belief affirmed by a necklace (and by the spiritist) a sense of confidence develops that enables the wearer to deal with adversity more positively, frontally. These objects of faith are also individualized by the spiritist for the particular emotional needs of the client, thus making their significance and perceived assistance greater.

Because the spiritist is perceived as sharing in the beliefs surrounding spiritism and its means, the client can share a deep spiritual-emotional phenomenon which occurs to him or her and not feel ridiculed. (This phenomenon, deeply related to one's own feelings or unconscious, is perceived as belonging to a "third kind" of being, which affects one, but is not one, or one's self. This enables clients to deal in many cases more objectively with one's subjective realm.)

The spiritist system is used to establish an accepting atmosphere with the client. This allows more clinical material to emerge as a result of increased trust. In a sense, the fact that both spiritist and client believe in the "objects of faith" enables both to become clearly and specifically engaged in the process of improving the client's mental health. The use of external objects facilitates the therapeutic relationship between client and spiritist. The use of spiritually-empowered external means for improvement or protection deflects the usual feelings of anger, hostility or love that patients evolve toward therapists. This allows spiritist and client to focus on the client's relationships with significant others.

The patient-therapist relationship is not used as a model or testing ground to resolve problems with others. The relationship with the spiritist tends to be more a relationship with another means by which the client may "get better," or rid himself of "evil spirits." The spiritist is another means for faith-support. The spiritist expands the client's self-awareness and ego-strength without entering into a heavy psychological relationship with the client. He maintains his position as a mediator/medium. Negatives are attributed to a third force, a spiritual force beyond both client and spiritist. This convenient third party absorbs negative feelings (of guilt, hostility, anger) generally elicited in analysis and often attributed to or absorbed by the client and/or the therapist.

Goals of Psychotherapy and Spiritism

There are fundamental similarities between the goals of the psychotherapist and the spiritist. In terms of the treatment technique, they both start out by accepting the client's version of reality. For example, the psychotherapist listens to a client complain that he is not sufficiently loved by his spouse. The therapist accepts it at face value. If the same client were to visit a spiritist, he would be listened to in the same supportive manner. However, as the treatment progresses, the psychotherapist and the spiritist handle the client differently. These different approaches are rooted in the philosophical differences in each of the systems. In psychotherapy, the belief is that the client contributes to his own problems by virtue of his negative behavior as he interacts with others. Part of the process of psychotherapy is to analyze the client's behavior and to explore alternative ways of interacting with others more positively. Essentially, the client must, at some point, assume the responsibility for both his demonstrable behavior and the consequences of that behavior. The spiritist, on the other hand, continues to stand with the client in a coalition against the externalized third party: *el espíritu malo* (the bad spirit).

Thus, in psychotherapy, the client is put in touch with his hostile feelings towards others. The spiritist attributes these negative feelings to a disembodied other (the bad spirit), thus relieving the client of the anxiety of responsibility. Moreover, the spiritist contacts the sources of ego-strength, *las protecciones y los guías* (the good protecting spirits and the spirit guides), that are culturally available for the client. In fact, the very process, which has been likened to psychodrama, of getting in touch with the positive spirits allows the client to integrate the positive ego-strength easily in an accepting cultural environment. Even the process of educating a poorly-developed spirit *(dándole luz al espíritu)* is essentially a non-threatening therapeutic technique practiced by spiritists which gets the client in touch with the negative aspects of his self-concept.

In the end, despite differences in treatment techniques, both the spiritist and psychotherapist help the client to feel better. The fundamental difference between psychotherapy and spiritism is that the spiritist, to paraphrase William Ryan, the psychologist, does not blame the victim.

Perhaps because the island of Puerto Rico was historically occupied so often militarily, the inhabitants began to feel that power in all its forms lay outside their control. This is not to say that Puerto Rican culture is psychotic or paranoid. It is a plausible illustration of how the Puerto Rican world view, *el ay bendito*, fits the spiritist system.

Traditional psychotherapy, with its constant insistence that the client must recognize his hostile feelings and accept responsibility, may well be emotionally upsetting to the Puerto Rican client. This does not mean that the therapist should change his therapeutic goals. It does mean that he has to time his interventions judiciously so as not to drive the client out of therapy. It also means that he has to be culturally aware enough to respect the belief system of his client. What is needed is not wholesale, indiscriminate aping of spiritist techniques for psychotherapeutic purposes. Instead, careful investigation by qualified bilingual/bicultural psychotherapists is necessary in order to create new, effective therapeutic approaches which maintain the dignity and self-worth of Puerto Rican clients.

Card Reading

One of the things a spiritist will do in a *consulta*, i.e., a session, is to read the cards; a pack of Spanish playing cards is normally used. He interprets the cards in a narrative fashion. In order to clarify or focus clearly on the specifics of the client's problem, the spiritist may manipulate the ambiguity inherent in the symbolism of each card. He achieves this by asking the client questions as the reading progresses.

After a thorough study of a number of medieval divinatory manuals, and training with a spiritualist, I developed a unique way of reading cards. I have found correspondences between the symbols of each card and a psychoanalytically-oriented dynamism.

There are 22 illustrated Tarot cards, but only 10 of them chosen at random can be laid out in sequence at any one reading.[2] Traditionally, each of the 22 cards has its own meaning. Each of the 10 positions has been traditionally assigned a specific meaning as well. Let us take for example Tarot card number 13. It presents the forbidding figure of a skeleton armed with a murderous-looking scythe.

Traditionally, it represents Death. Card number 12 is illustrated by the figure of a man hung by one of his feet in an upside-down position. Traditionally, this card is interpreted as Sacrifice.

The seventh position is traditionally a symbol for the client him/herself. Likewise, the eighth position traditionally represents the environmental factors surrounding the client. I have reinterpreted all of the 22 Tarot cards. I have also reinterpreted the 10 positions in the sequence. By way of illustrating how this new system relates to psychotherapeutic technique, I will give my reinterpretations of both cards and both positions. One of the areas of concern in psychotherapy is the love relationship of the client. With this in mind, card number 13 in my system signifies a major restructuring of the love relationship and the anxiety growing out of the interpersonal friction which that demand puts on the relationship. Card number 12 in my system reveals the psychological attitude or mood of the client relative to his/her love partner. The eighth card in my system discloses the psychological reaction of the client's love partner to him/her.

In a reading where card number 13 falls in the seventh position and card number 12 falls in the eighth position, I have interpreted the client as demanding a radical restructuring of the way in which the client and his/her partner interact in the love relationship. On the other hand, the partner's ambivalent feelings about the client result in the partner's inability to make a decision to change in ways which can accommodate the client. What can be deduced from this is that a separation or divorce may be imminent. The fears and anxieties surrounding those possibilities become grist for the therapeutic mill.

Although these two cards represent only a small part of the total 10-card sequence and of the entire set of 22, their interpretation focuses immediately upon one of the major interpersonal relationships in the life of the client. It encourages him/her to discuss his feelings openly in the very first psychotherapy session. In fact, the reading begins the process of therapy. It leaves something, to paraphrase Hemingway, for the client to explore when he/she returns for a second session. This approach motivates the client to remain in therapy at the very point when most clients normally drop out: after the very first encounter with a clinician.

Card reading achieves the same psychotherapeutic purpose as a projective test. In the projective test, the impressions of the client are verbalized as a response to the stimulus presented. In the card reading, the practice of having the answers come from another source outside the patient confirms his initial self-diagnosis and validates his own feelings. The process of interpretation and the subsequent question-and-answer dialogue which emerges as a result of the reading is very much in keeping with the initial interview procedures used by most clinically-oriented mental-health professionals.

Course of Spiritist Therapy

Initially, the client comes to the spiritist or psychotherapist feeling that the professional has the answers to his problems. The initial use of the card reading, with its emphasis on the therapist doing most of the talking while administering the reading, helps to cement this initial feeling on the part of the client. In the initial stages of therapy, this is beneficial because the therapist's knowledge of spiritist dogma and his acceptance of the phenomena as being valid for the client helps to establish the necessary trust that is essential if the therapist is to actively encourage the client to remain in therapy beyond the initial interview. This phenomenological acceptance of the experience that the patient brings into therapy with him is what Binswanger, Boss and May refer to when they talk of the therapist's being-in-the-world with his patient, of sharing his feelings through the process of empathy.[3]

The purpose of using any therapeutic technique is to increase the mental well-being of the client. It is used as part of the therapeutic process by which the client learns to recognize his own emotional strengths. In order to achieve this, the therapist must be in touch with the client's sources of ego strength. These sources of ego strength are located within the culture in which the client was reared. For Puerto Ricans, spiritism is a means through which ego strengths may be built and/or may surface.

When a client who holds spiritist beliefs comes to see a therapist, he is obviously looking for a vehicle to help him cope. It is not the task of therapists to replace their client's value system with their own. Neither should it be the aim of the analyst to make the client give up his spiritist beliefs—just as a therapist should/would not try to make an atheist out of a Jew or Catholic. The therapist must provide a means or mechanism which the client can use to help him solve the problems of life. Initially, the client sees the therapist as the proverbial answer man. Card-reading and familiarity with spiritist dogma helps to reinforce that perception. Therefore, it is the task of the therapist in the later stages of therapy to wean the client away from that perception and let him recognize and accept in himself the power that he holds over his own life. Praying to the spirits, lighting candles, taking herb baths are all adjuncts to, not substitutes for, his own strength.

It is part of the task of the therapist not only to help the client discover his options, but to help him through the anguish of having to accept responsibility for the consequences attached to his choices. The end result of spiritist therapy or any other kind of therapy should be that both spiritually and materially the client's life can be more productive for himself and for others.

In addition to the similarity in techniques employed by therapists and spiritists, there are some other interesting conceptual parallels. First in spiritism, there is the immateriality of one's Spirit which is said to influence human behavior. An interesting parallel can be found in the human emotions themselves, which are not quantifiable per se and which influence behavior. In each system, observable human behavior points to the likely existence of powerful entities — the Spirit in one, emotion in the other. Secondly, there is the concept of the cosmic universe peopled by dark spirits. In psychoanalysis, the concept of the unconscious with its powerful hidden instinctual forces is constantly used by the therapists. Thirdly, there is an odd similarity between the *id-ego-superego* components and their resultant dynamic balance and the spiritist concepts of bad spirits (*espíritus malos*), good spirits (*protección*) and guides (*guías*).

Both the spiritist and the therapist deal with powerful forces. Therapy with Puerto Rican patients can be more successful when the client's value system and his stockpile of cultural images can be incorporated by a sensitive, flexible therapist who can help make the person more self-reliant.

A Case History

The following case history, taken from my private practice as a psychoanalyst, helps to illustrate some of the psychoanalytic processes described above.

The patient is a 25-year-old Puerto Rican female who works as an executive secretary. Her parents are spiritists who have sessions at home. She was born in New York City but is both bilingual and bicultural. She does not claim to attend sessions now but attended while she lived at home. The patient now shares an apartment with a female roommate. Her psychosexual development included a sexual relationship when she was 19. She had an abortion at 20. The relationship ended soon after when the patient realized she was "being used sexually" by her boyfriend.

Her presenting symptom was that she was afraid to travel alone in the subway or bus. She was using this inability to travel as an excuse for her not being able to hold a job. At the time she came for therapy she had had three jobs in five months. She would find a friend who lived nearby or coax someone from her immediate family to shepherd her downtown. After several weeks, the person would get tired of being so important or needed and would beg off. As a result, the client would begin to call in sick. She would not return until someone would agree to ride down with her. Consequently, she lost job after job.

One day, after discussing the problem, she built up enough courage to try a solo trip. A few stops after she got on, she experienced such a fierce anxiety attack that she had to get off and call in sick. Her boss was incensed.

The card reading took place immediately after she discussed the spiritualist sessions her parents held at home. Quite naturally, she was hesitant to discuss her experience for fear of being ridiculed.

The initial card reading helped to focus on a decision she had to make. It also pointed up a discrepancy between her self-perception and her observable behavior. Stimulated by the card interpretations, she discussed her life decision. She was encouraged to express her own diagnosis, in her own terms. She assigned the root of her problem to an *espíritu de retraso*, an undeveloped spirit, who wanted to block her from bettering herself.

She was encouraged to continue the herb baths, prayers and special candles dedicated to her guardian spirit, or *protección*. At the same time, she was encouraged to use her conscious will to control the evil spirits. Once she gained confidence in her own ability to control the degree to which the spirits could influence her, we began to work on her ability to make choices. From there, she moved to accept the fact that choices have positive and negative consequences. Eventually, she gained control over her life as she made more choices that resulted in positive consequences.

Her dependency, which was the root of her subway phobia, diminished. Eventually, she was able to hold a permanent job and even earned a promotion. The patient also has a satisfactory heterosexual relationship with another man at the present time.

With time, she explained that the evil spirits could gain ascendancy over her when she allowed her conscious will to float. But when she grounded her free will in herself and in her responsibilities and the things that gave her pleasure, the spirits got weaker. In other words, when she took responsibility for her actions and acted independently, she felt less subject to her fears.

Obviously, the patient still held her spiritist beliefs, but she found her inner strength and tied it to a process that worked for her. To an extent, some of the faith she so abundantly possessed was transferred to another system: psychotherapy. This worked for her as did spiritism. The combined means did not diminish her trust in either herself or her spiritist beliefs.

NOTES

1. Spiritism is a term used throughout this paper to denote a codified belief system practiced by Puerto Ricans who believe in the existence of spirits which interact with human beings. The term spiritualism, on the other hand, is a more generic term which signifies an ethical concern with moral qualities, such as honesty. It also connotes a rejection of the usual pecuniary motives which drive most human beings.

2. The entire Tarot deck consists of 22 cards called the Major Arcanum and another 56 cards called the Minor Arcanum. For psychotherapeutic purposes, I have reinterpreted only the 22 cards of the Major Arcanum.

3. Ludwig Binswanger, a Swiss psychiatrist who trained under C.G. Jung, another giant in the field, was a contemporary of Sigmund Freud, the father of psychoanalysis. Binswanger and Freud mutually respected each other as professionals, and developed a long-lasting friendship. However, they had deep philosophical differences. Freud felt that only a dispassionate objective analyst who interpreted the client's behavior from an emotionally-detached vantage point could be a successful psychotherapist.

Binswanger, on the other hand, was dramatically opposed to that stance. He believed that only when the psychotherapist accepts as valid the client's perception of himself and his world, and only when the therapist enters that world emotionally through empathy, can the therapeutic treatment be successful. Many modern psychoanalysts, notably Rollo May, an American, and Medard Boss, a German, have followed Binswanger's cue and have written extensively on the theoretical and practical implications for psychotherapeutic treatment engendered by his philosophical stance. (Cf. References for citation of May's work, which includes contributions by Binswanger and May. The references also contain the citation of Boss' own work.)

REFERENCES

Boss, Medard. Psychoanalysis and Daseinsanalysis. Trans. Ludwig B. Lefebre. New York: Basic Books. 1963.

Garrison, Vivian. "Spiritism: Implications for provision of mental health services to Puerto Rican populations." Unpublished paper read at the Eighth Annual Meeting of the Southern Anthropological Society, Columbia, MO, February 24-26. 1972.

Kardec, Allan. El Libro de los Espíritus. New York: Studium Corporation. 1975a.

El Libro de los Mediums. New York: Studium Corporation. 1975b.

Matos Paoli, Francisco. Canto de la Locura. San Juan, Puerto Rico: Instituto de Cultura Puertorriqueña. 1976.

May, Rollo, Ernest Angel, and Henri Ellenberger, eds. Existence: A New Dimension in Psychology. New York: Basic Books. 1958.

Rogler, Lloyd H. and Hollingshead, August B. Trapped: Families and Schizophrenia. New York: John Wiley and Sons. 1965.

Bibliography

Acosta, U. (1987). *New Voices of Old: Five Centuries of Puerto Rican Cultural History*. Santurce, P.R.: Permanent Press.

Acosta-Belén, E., ed. (1979). *The Puerto Rican Woman*. New York: Praeger. (revised edition 1986).

Acosta-Belén, E., and B. Sjostrom, eds. (1988). *The Hispanic Experience in the U.S.* New York: Praeger.

Acosta-Belén, E. (1992). Beyond Island Boundaries: Ethnicity, Gender, and Cultural Revitalization in Nuyorican Literature. *Callaloo*, 15(4),979–998.

Acosta-Belén, E., & V. Sánchez Korrol (1993). *Jesús Colón: The Way It Was and Other Writings*. Houston, Tex.: Arte Público Press.

Aliotta, J.J. (1991). *The Puerto Ricans*. New York: Chelsea House Publishers.

Alvarez, C., A. Bennett, M. Greenless, P. Pedraza, & A. Pousada (1988). *Speech and Ways of Speaking in a Bilingual Puerto Rican Community*. New York: Centro de Estudios Puertorriqueños, Hunter College, City University of New York.

Attinasi, J., P. Pedraza, S. Poplack, & A. Pousada (1988). *Intergenerational Perspectives on Bilingualism*. New York: Centro de Estudios Puertorriqueños, Hunter College, City University of New York.

Babín, M.T. (1971). *The Puerto Ricans' Spirit: Their History, Life and Culture*. New York: Collier Books.

Baver, S. (1984). Puerto Rican Politics in New York City: The Post–World War II Period. In J. Jennings & M. Rivera, eds., *Puerto Rican Politics in Urban America*, pp. 43–59. Westport, Conn.: Greenwood Press.

Bean, C. (1974). *My name is José*. Chicago: Herald Press (1434 W. 51 St. 60609).

Bean, F., & M. Tienda (1988). *The Hispanic Population in the U.S.* New York: Russell Sage Foundation.

Benmayor, R., A. Juarbe, C. Alvarez, & B. Vásquez (1987). *Stories to*

Live By: Continuity and Change in Three Generations of Puerto Rican Women. Working paper, Centro de Estudios Puertorriqueños, Hunter College, New York.

Benmayor, R., R.M. Torruellas, & A.L. Juarbe (1992). *Responses to Poverty among Puerto Rican Women: Identity, Community and Cultural Citizenship.* New York: Centro de Estudios Puertorriqueños, Hunter College, City University of New York.

Berle, B. (1958). *80 Puerto Rican Families in New York City.* New York: Columbia University Press.

Bloomfield, R. (1985). *Puerto Rico: The Search for a National Policy.* Boulder, Colo.: Westview Press.

Bonilla-Santiago, G. (1988). *Organizing Puerto Rican Migrant Farmworkers: The Experience of Puerto Ricans in New Jersey.* New York: Lang.

Bonilla, F., & R. Campos (1986). *Industry and Idleness.* New York: Centro de Estudios Puertorriqueños, Hunter College, CUNY.

Burgos, W., H. Rodríguez-Vecchini, & C.A. Torre (1993). *The Commuter Nation: Perspectives on Puerto Rican Migration.* San Juan, P.R.: Editorial de la Universidad de Puerto Rico.

Cafferty San Juan, P., & C. Rivera-Martínez (1981c). *The Politics of Language: The Dilemma of Bilingual Education for Puerto Ricans.* Boulder, Colo.: Westview Press.

Calvo Ospina, Hernando (1995). *Salsa! Havana Heat, Bronx Beat.* New York: Monthly Review Press (distributor).

Cardona, L.A. (1974). *The Coming of the Puerto Ricans.* Washington: Unidos.

Carr, R. (1984). *Puerto Rico: A Colonial Experiment.* New York: New York University Press.

Chenault, L.R. (1938). *The Puerto Rican Migrant in New York City.* New York: Columbia University Press. (Reissued Russell and Russell, 1970).

Colón, J. (1982). *A Puerto Rican in New York and Other Sketches.* New York: International Publishers.

Cooper, P. (1972). *Growing up Puerto Rican.* New York: Arbor House.

Cordasco, F., & E. Bucchioni (1973). *The Puerto Rican Experience: A Sociological Sourcebook.* Totowa, N.J.: Rowman & Littlefield.

Cultural Studies Task Force (1987). *Aprender a Luchar, Luchar es Aprender.* New York: Centro de Estudios Puertorriqueños, Hunter College, City University of New York.

De la Garza, R., L. Desipio, C. García, J. García, & A. Falcón (1992). *Latino Voices: Mexican, Puerto Rican, and Cuban Perspectives on American Politics.* Boulder, Colo.: Westview Press.

Díaz-Stevens, A.M. (1993). *Oxcart Catholicism On Fifth Avenue.* Notre Dame, Ind.: University of Notre Dame Press.

Estades, R. (1978). *Patterns of Political Participation of Puerto Ricans in New York City.* (translated and printed in Spanish) Rio Piedras, P.R.: Editorial Universitaria, Universidad de Puerto Rico.

Falcón, A. (1984). An Introduction to the Literature of Puerto Rican Politics in Urban America. In J. Jennings & M. Rivera, eds., *Puerto Rican Politics in Urban America,* pp. 145–154. Westport, Conn.: Greenwood Press.

Fernández, R. (1988). *Los Macheteros: The Violent Struggle for Puerto Rican Independence.* Westport, Conn.: Greenwood.

Fernández, R. (1992). *The Disenchanted Island: Puerto Rico and the United States in the Twentieth Century.* New York: Praeger.

Figueroa, J. (1989). *Survival on the Margin: A Documentary Study of the Underground Economy in a Puerto Rican Ghetto.* New York: Vantage Press.

Figueroa, L. (1974). *History of Puerto Rico.* New York: Anaya.

Fishman, J.A., R.L. Cooper, & R. Ma (1971). *Bilingualism in the barrio.* Bloomington: University of Indiana Press.

Fitzpatrick, J.P., Rev. (1966). Oscar Lewis and the Puerto Rican Family. *America,* 115:778–779 (December 10, 1966).

Fitzpatrick, J.P., Rev. (1971). *Puerto Rican Americans.* Englewood Cliffs, N.J.: Prentice-Hall, Inc. (Revised edition 1987).

Flores, J., ed. (1987) *Divided Arrival: Narratives of the Puerto Rican Migration, 1920–50.* New York: Centro de Estudios Puertorriqueños, Hunter College, City University of New York.

Flores, J. (1993). *Divided Borders: Essays on Puerto Rican Identity.* Houston, Tex.: Arte Público Press.

Friedlander, S.L. (1965). *Labor Migration and Economic Growth.* Boston, Mass.: The MIT Press.

García Coll, C. & M. Mattei (1989). *The Psychosocial Development of Puerto Rican Women.* Westport, Conn.: Praeger Publishers.

Glazer, N. & D.P. Moynihan (1970). *Beyond the Melting Pot* (2nd ed.). Cambridge, Mass.: MIT Press.

Guarnaccia, P., V. De La Cancela, & E. Carrillo (1989). "The Multiple Meanings of Ataques de Nervios in the Latino Community, *Medical Anthropology,* II:47–62.

Handlin, O. (1959). *The Newcomers: Negroes and Puerto Ricans in a Changing Metropolis.* Cambridge, Mass.: Harvard University

Press.

Hardy-Fanta, C. (1992). *Latina Politics: Latino Politics.* Philadelphia: Temple University Press.

Harris, W. W. (1980). *Puerto Rico's Fighting 65th U.S. Infantry: From San Juan to Chorwan.* San Rafael, Cal.: Presidio Press.

Harwood, A. (1977). *Rx-spiritist as needed: A Study of a Puerto Rican Community Mental Health Resource.* New York: Wiley.

Haslip-Viera, G., & S. Baver (forthcoming). *Latinos in New York: A Community in Transition.* Notre Dame, Indiana: University of Notre Dame Press.

Heine, J. (1983). *Time for Decision: The United States and Puerto Rico.* Lanham, Md.: North-South Publishing Co.

Hernández, J. (1967). *Return Migration to Puerto Rico.* Berkeley, Cal.: University of California Press.

Hernández, J. (1983c). *Puerto Rican Youth Employment.* Maplewood, N.J.: Waterfront Press.

Hernández, J. (1992). *Conquered Peoples in America.* (4th ed.). Dubuque, Iowa: Kendall/Hunt Publishing Co.

Hidalgo, H., & J.L. McEniry (1985). *Hispanic Temas: A Contribution to the Knowledge Bank of the Hispanic Community.* Newark, N.J.: Rutgers, The State University of New Jersey, Puerto Rican Studies Program.

History Task Force (1979). *Labor Migration Under Capitalism.* New York: Monthly Review Press.

History Task Force (1983). *Sources for the Study of Puerto Rican Migration 1879–1930.* New York: Centro de Estudios Puertorriqueños, Hunter College, City University of New York.

Iglesias, C.A., ed. (1984). *Memoirs of Bernardo Vega.* New York: Monthly Review Press.

Isasi-Díaz, Ada María and Yolanda Tarango (1988). *Hispanic Women: Prophetic Voice in the Church.* San Francisco: Harper & Row, Publishers, Inc.

Jennings, J. & Rivera, M. (1984). *Puerto Rican Politics in Urban America.* Westport, Conn.: Greenwood Press.

Jordan, Howard (1994). "The New York Puerto Rican Parade," *Crítica,* July, Number 2, pp. 3–11.

Lamberty, G., & C. García Coll (1994). *Puerto Rican Women and Children: Issues in Health, Growth, and Development.* New York: Plenum.

Language Policy Task Force (1978). Language Policy and the Puerto Rican Community. New York: Hunter College, Centro de

Estudios Puertorriqueños.

Language Policy Task Force (1980). Social Dimensions of Language Use in East Harlem. New York: Hunter College, Centro de Estudios Puertorriqueños.

Language Policy Task Force (1982). Intergenerational Perspectives on Bilingualism: From Community to Classroom. New York: Hunter College, Centro de Estudios Puertorriqueños.

Lauria-Perricelli, A. (1990). A Study in Historical and Critical Anthropology: The Making of The People of Puerto Rico. Ann Arbor: University Microfilms.

Levins Morales, A., & R. Morales (1986). Getting Home Alive. Ithaca: Firebrand Books.

Lewis, O. (1966). La Vida: A Puerto Rican Family in the Culture of Poverty—San Juan and New York. New York: Random House.

López, A. (1973). The Puerto Rican Papers. New York: Bobbs-Merrill.

López, A. (1987). Doña Licha's Island: Modern Colonialism in Puerto Rico. Boston: South End Press.

López, A. (1980). The Puerto Ricans: Their History, Culture and Society. Cambridge, Mass.: Schenkman Pub. Co.

López, A., & J. Petras, eds. (1974). Puerto Rico and Puerto Ricans. Cambridge, Mass: Schenkman Publishing Co.

Maldonado, A.A. (1984). Portraits of the Puerto Rican Experience. IPRUS, 384 E. 149 St., Bronx, N.Y. (edited by Louis Reyes Rivera, Julio Rodríguez, Carlos de Jesús.)

Maldonado Denis, M. (1967). Oscar Lewis, La Vida, y la enajena-cion. Revista de Ciencias Sociales, 11(2),253–59.

Maldonado Denis, M. (1972). Puerto Rico: A Socio-Historic Inter-pretation. New York: Random House.

Maldonado Denis, M. (1980). The Emigration Dialectic: Puerto Rico and the U.S.A. New York: International Publishers.

Mapp, E. (1974). Puerto Rican Perspectives. Metuchen: The Scare-crow Press.

Martell Otero, Loida I. (1994). En Las Manos del Señor: Ministry in the Hispanic American Context. The Appleseed. 1.1 (winter) pp. 14–21.

Martínez, A. (1974). Rising Voices. New York: New American Library.

Martínez, A. (1988). "The Effects of Acculturation and Racial Identity on Self-Esteem and Psychological Well-Being Among Young Puerto Ricans." Doctoral dissertation, City University of New York.

McLuhan, T.C. (1972). Touch the Earth. New York: Pocketbooks.

Meléndez, E., C.E. Rodríguez, & J. Barry Figueroa (1991). *Hispanics in the Labor Force: Issues and Policies*. New York: Plenum Press.

Meléndez, E., & E. Meléndez (1993). *Colonial Dilemma: Critical Perspectives on Contemporary Puerto Rico*. Boston, Mass.: South End Press.

Meyer, Gerald (1989) *Vito Marcantonio: Radical Politician, 1902–1954*. Albany, N.Y.: State University Press.

Mills, C.W., C. Senior, & R. Goldsen (1950). *The Puerto Rican Journey: New York's Newest Migrants*. New York: Harper & Bros.

Morales, J. (1986). *Puerto Rican Poverty and Migration: We Just Had to Try Elsehere*. New York: Praeger.

Morales-Carrión, A. (1983). *Puerto Rico: A Political and Cultural History*. New York: W.W. Norton.

Morales-Dorta, J. (1976). *Puerto Rican Espiritismo: Religion and Psychotherapy*. New York: Vantage Press.

Nieves, J. (1987). Puerto Rican Studies: Roots and Challenges. In M. Sánchez & A. Stevens-Arroyo, eds., *Toward a Renaissance of Puerto Rican Studies*, pp. 3–12. Boulder, Colo.: Social Science Monographs, Atlantic Research and Publications, Inc., Highland Lakes, N.J., distributed by Columbia University Press.

Oral History Task Force. (1986). *Extended roots: From Hawaii to New York*. New York: Centro de Estudios Puertorriqueños, Hunter College, City University of New York.

Ortiz, A., ed. (forthcoming). *Puerto Rican Women and Work*. Philadelphia: Temple University Press.

Ortiz Cofer (1993). *The Latin Deli*. New York: W.W. Norton & Co.

Padilla, E. (1958). *Up from Puerto Rico*. New York: Columbia University Press.

Padilla, F. (1985). *Latino Ethnic Consciousness: The Case of Mexican-Americans and Puerto Ricans in Chicago*. Notre Dame, Ind.: University of Notre Dame Press.

Padilla, F. (1987). *Puerto Rican Chicago*, Notre Dame, Ind.: University of Notre Dame Press.

Padilla, Felix (1990). "Salsa: Puerto Rican and Latino Music," in *Journal of Popular Culture*, 24:1:(Summer):87–104.

Padilla, F. (1992). *The Gang as an American Enterprise*. New Brunswick, N.J.: Rutgers University Press.

Padilla, F., & L. Santiago (1993). *Outside the Wall: The Struggle of a Puerto Rican Prisoner's Wife*. New Brunswick: Rutgers

University Press.

Pedraza, P. (1987). *An Ethnographic Analysis of Language Use in the Puerto Rican Community of East Harlem*. New York: Centro de Estudios Puertorriqueños, Hunter College, City University of New York.

Pérez y González, María E. (1993). *Latinas in Ministry: A Pioneering Study on Women Minister, Educators and Students of Theology*. New York: New York City Mission Society.

Pérez y Mena, A.I. (1991) *Speaking with the Dead: Development of Afro-Latin Religion among Puerto Ricans in the United States*. New York: AMS Press.

Rand, C. (1958). *The Puerto Ricans*. New York: Oxford University Press.

Reynolds, R.M., C. Rodríguez–Fraticcelli, & B. Vásquez Erazo (1989). *Campus in Bondage: A 1948 Microcosm of Puerto Rico in Bondage*. New York: Centro de Estudios Puertorriqueños, Hunter College, City University of New York.

Ribes Tovar, F. (1968). *Handbook of the Puerto Rican Community*. Puerto Rico: Libro.

Ríos, Palmira (1985). "Puerto Rican Women in the United States Labor Market," *Line of March*, 18 (Fall).

Ribes Tovar, F. (1970). *Enciclopedia Puertorriquena Ilustrada: The Puerto Rican Heritage Encyclopedia*. New York: Plus Ultra Educational Publishers.

Rivera-Batiz and Carlos Santiago (1994). *Puerto Ricans in the United States: A Changing Reality*. Washington, D.C.: National Puerto Rican Coalition.

Rodríguez, C.E. (1974). *The Ethnic Queue: The Case of Puerto Ricans*. San Francisco, Cal.: R & E Research Associates.

Rodríguez, C.E. (1989). *Puerto Ricans: Born in the USA*. Boston: Unwin & Hyman. (Reissued by Westview Press in Boulder, Colo. in 1991.)

Rodríguez, C.E. (1994). Challenging the Racial Hegemony: Puerto Ricans in the U.S. In R. Sanjek & S. Gregory, S., eds. *Everyone's Business: The Politics of Race and Identity*. New Brunswick: Rutgers University Press.

Rodríguez, C.E. (1995). Puerto Ricans in Historical and Social Science Research. In J.A. Banks & C.A. McGee Banks, eds., *Handbook of Research on Multicultural Education*. New York: Macmillan.

Rodríguez, C.E. (forthcoming). Racial Themes in the Literature. In

G. Haslip-Viera & S. Baver, eds., *Latinos in New York: A Community in Transition*. Notre Dame, Ind.: University of Notre Dame Press.

Rodríguez, C.E. (forthcoming). *Latin Looks: Latino Images in the Media*. Boulder, Co.: Westview Press.

Rodríguez, C., V. Sánchez Korrol, & O. Alers (1980c, 1984). *The Puerto Rican Struggle: Essays on Survival in the U.S.* Maplewood, N.J.: Waterfront Press.

Rodríguez de Laguna, A. (1987). *Images and Identities: The Puerto Rican in Two World Contexts*. New Brunswick, N.J.: Transaction Books.

Rogler, L.H. (1972). *Migrant in the City: The Life of a Puerto Rican Action Group*. New York: Basic Books.

Rogler, L.H. & Santana Cooney, R. (1984). *Puerto Rican Families in New York City: Intergenerational Processes*. Maplewood, N.J.: Waterfront Press.

Sánchez, M.E., and A. Stevens-Arroyo, eds. (1987). *Toward a Renaissance of Puerto Rican Studies: Ethnic and Area Studies in University Education*. Boulder, Colo.: Social Science Monographs: Higland Lakes, N.J.: Atlantic Research and Publications.

Sánchez-Korrol, V. (1994). *From Colonia to Community: The History of Puerto Ricans in New York City*. Berkeley, Cal.: University of California Press. (First edition 1983. Westport, Conn.: Greenwood Press).

Sánchez Korrol, V. (1993). In Search of Unconventional Women: Histories of Puerto Rican Women in Religious Vocations before Mid-Century. In Nancy F. Cott, ed., *History of Women in the United States*. Munich, Germany: K.G. Saur.

Sánchez Korrol, V. (forthcoming). Towards Bilingual Education: Puerto Rican Women Educators and the New York City Schools, 1947–1968. In Altagracia Ortiz, ed., *Puerto Rican Women and Work*. Philadelphia: Temple University Press.

Sandis, E., ed. (1970). *The Puerto Rican experience*. New York: Selected Academic Readings.

Santiago, Esmeralda (1994). *When I Was Puerto Rican*. New York: Vintage Books.

Santiago, Roberto (1995). *Boricuas: Influential Puerto Rican Writings—An Anthology*. New York: Ballantine Books.

Senior, C. (1961). *Strangers, Then Neighbors: From Pilgrims to Puerto Ricans*. New York: Freedom Books.

Sexton Cayo, P. (1965). *Spanish Harlem*. New York: Harper & Row.

Sheehan, S. (1976). *A Welfare Mother*. Boston: Houghton Mifflin.

Steiner, S. (1974). *The Islands: The Worlds of the Puerto Ricans*. New York: Harper & Row.

Stevens-Arroyo, A.M., and Ana María Díaz-Stevens (1994). *An Enduring Flame: Studies on Latino Popular Religiosity*. New York: The Bildner Center. The Graduate School and University Center of the City University of New York.

Thomas, P. (1967). *Down These Mean Streets*. New York: Knopf.

Torres, A. (1994). *Between Melting Pot and Mosaic: African Americans and Puerto Ricans in the New York Political Economy*. Philadelphia, Penna.: Temple University Press.

Torres, A., & C.E. Rodríguez (1991). Latino Research and Policy: the Puerto Rican Case. In E. Meléndez, C.E. Rodríguez, & J. Barry Figueroa, eds., *Hispanics in the Labor Force: Issues and Policies*, pp. 247–263. New York: Plenum Press.

Torruellas, R.M., R. Benmayor, A. Goris, & A.L. Juarbe (1991). Affirming cultural citizenship in the Puerto Rican community. New York: Centro de Estudios Puertorriqueños, Hunter College, City University of New York.

Torruellas, L.M., and J.L. Vásquez (1984). *Puertorriqueños que regresaron: Un analisis de su participación laboral*. Rio Piedras, P.R.: University of Puerto Rico.

U.S. Commission on Civil Rights (1976). *Puerto Ricans in the Continental United States: An Uncertain Future*. Washington, D.C.: A Report of the United States Commission on Civil Rights.

U.S. Dept. of Labor, Bureau of Labor Statistics (1995a). "A CPS Supplement for Testing Methods for Collecting Racial and Ethnic Information," May 1995 report. Washington, D.C.

U.S. Office of Management and Budget (1995). "Standards for the Classification of Federal Data on Race and Ethnicity; Notice," *Federal Register*, August 28, 1995, 60:166:44673–44693.

U.S. Department of Commerce, Bureau of the Census (1995b). "1996 Race and Ethnic Targeted Test; Notice," Part XII, *Federal Register*, December 1, 1995, 60:231:(December):62010–62015.

Vázquez, J.M. (1992). Embattled Scholars in the Academy. *Callaloo*, 15(4),1039–1051.

Wagenheim, Kal (1975). *A Survey of Puerto Ricans on the U.S. Mainland in the 1970s*. New York: Praeger Publishers.

Wagenheim, K., & O. Jiménez de Wagenheim (1973). *The Puerto Ricans: A Documentary History*. New York: Praeger. Updated edition, 1997, Princeton: Markus Wiener Publishers.

Wakefield, D. (1959). *Island in the City: The World of Spanish Harlem*. Boston: Houghton Mifflin. (Reprinted by Arno Press, New York, 1975.)

Walsh, K. (1991). *The Struggle for Voice: Issues of Language, Power and Schooling for Puerto Ricans*. New York: Bergin & Garvey.

Young Lords Party. (1971). *Palante: Young Lords Party*. New York: McGraw Hill Publishing Co.

Zentella, A.C. (1994). *Growing up Bilingual: Puerto Rican Children in New York*. London, Cambridge: Basil/Blackwell.

Zitko, Joanne, & Gustavo Collins (1994). *The 1994–95 Salsa Club Directory*, available from Zitko/Collins, P.O. Box 671, New York, N.Y. 10025-0671.